Praise for
A Novice's Guide to Speaking in Public

"This is a remarkably insightful guide to giving successful presentations or speeches—something we all need help with, no matter our level of familiarity. Given Dr. Faulkner's 40+ years of presentation experience to C-level executives, I only wish that he had written this book first in his prolific career because I needed this advice ten years ago! So, don't hesitate to perfect your whole presentation—read it today!"

—**Kevin Noonan**, Sr. Consultant, NBCUniversal

"At some time in our lives, nearly all of us will be called upon to give a speech of some sort. Whether it be a wedding toast or a business presentation, a seminar or a eulogy, we all want to do a good job and not embarrass ourselves in the process. In *A Novice's Guide to Speaking in Public*, Michael Faulkner provides sensible, easy-to-follow guidelines on how to make sure that whatever presentation you might give will be interesting and effectively delivered. If you are an infrequent public speaker, this book is definitely for you. And, if you are an experienced presenter, you will find valuable tips to help you be even better. Bravo, Dr. Faulkner—finally a book on public speaking for the rest of us.

—**Steven Isaac**, Former CEO, Forbes Education, and Founding CEO, Education Dynamics

"Read this book. Dr. Faulkner is a dear friend of mine. He speaks. People listen."

—**Richard Vincent Kelly**, NCW

"'You need the right tools to do the right job' is a phrase we hear all too often. And as a master craftsman in his field, Michael Faulkner empties his toolbox of wisdom out for all to see. The ten things you will learn here will demand and command the attention of your audience. This book is a must-have for presenters and speech givers; period!"

—**Dan Barr**, M.A., B.S.

"Like he has in his other books, Dr. Faulkner is able to draw on his vast education, life experiences, and work history to create easy-to-understand and concise information on complex topics. Dr. Faulkner's books and teachings have helped me to better myself and strive for maximum potential out of a small start-up business."

—**Eliot Spindel**

"Bon voyage to the plague of public speaking! Dr. Faulkner is a prolific writer, meticulous researcher, and ardent pragmatist with a can-opener aptitude for dissecting and conquering problems. His academic, military, and corporate experience are here married to common sense. This book will transform the quality of your talks with strategies proven under fire."

—**Ken Boyer**, English Professor (Retired), St. Louis Community College/FV

"We often hear the quote 'begin with the end in mind,' and this couldn't be more relevant when it comes to public speaking. Dr. Faulkner does a great job of breaking down a presentation into ten easy steps in order to overcome and harness the fear that comes with public speaking. In the end, you'll walk away with tips to tactfully and successfully engage any audience!"

—**Kristine Lester**, Marketing Manager in Higher Education field

A Novice's Guide to Speaking in Public

A Novice's Guide to Speaking in Public

10 Steps to Help You Succeed in
Your Next Presentation...
Without Years of Training!

Michael Lawrence Faulkner

Publisher: Paul Boger
Editor-in-Chief: Amy Neidlinger
Editorial Assistant: Olivia Basegio
Cover Designer: Chuti Prasertsith
Managing Editor: Kristy Hart
Project Editor: Elaine Wiley
Copy Editor: Geneil Breeze
Proofreader: Laura Hernandez
Indexer: Lisa Stumpf
Senior Compositor: Gloria Schurick
Manufacturing Buyer: Dan Uhrig

For information about buying this title in bulk quantities, or for special sales opportunities (which may include electronic versions; custom cover designs; and content particular to your business, training goals, marketing focus, or branding interests), please contact our corporate sales department at corpsales@pearsoned.com or (800) 382-3419.

For government sales inquiries, please contact governmentsales@pearsoned.com.

For questions about sales outside the U.S., please contact international@pearsoned.com.

Company and product names mentioned herein are the trademarks or registered trademarks of their respective owners.

Printed in the United States of America

First Printing October 2015

ISBN-10: 0-13-419386-5
ISBN-13: 978-0-13-419386-1

Pearson Education LTD.
Pearson Education Australia PTY, Limited
Pearson Education Singapore, Pte. Ltd.
Pearson Education Asia, Ltd.
Pearson Education Canada, Ltd.
Pearson Educación de Mexico, S.A. de C.V.
Pearson Education—Japan
Pearson Education Malaysia, Pte. Ltd.

Library of Congress Control Number: 2015946547

For Jo-Ann.

Throughout most of my adult life I have coached, taught, counseled, and advised thousands of people on how to communicate better. Yet, without a word she can leave me speechless.

Contents

Foreword

When Dr. Mike told me that he was going to write a book on presentation and public speaking skills, I was elated. He is the master of the podium!

"Get them on their feet and cheering" is what I thought after reading his latest book, which you are holding in your hand or electronic device right now.

You are in for a real treat. Dr. Michael Faulkner has condensed all the fundamentals of becoming a great speaker into what is almost the modern day's Cliff's Notes, as only he can do. After reading this easy-to-read and chock-full-of-substance book, you will walk away with practical skills to implement immediately, enjoy the whole process, and be richer for the experience.

Having known Dr. Mike for more years than each of us will admit to, I have had the great privilege of co-authoring three books with him and have read many of his other brilliant and thought provoking works. By the way, he has written so many wonderful books that I have often thought he should have his own library to house them all in.

Whether you are preparing for your next presentation and just want to "get through it" or if you are a seasoned professional and looking for a fantastic refresher on the do's, don'ts, and basics of a great presentation, you've come to the right place.

I guarantee you will be ear-marking page after page of this substantial and enlightening book. To any of us reading it, this book is impressive because of all the knowledge that Dr. Faulkner puts on every page. I was in awe of how he carefully traces every step in a concise yet analytical and methodical way.

Enjoy it and learn.

Andrea R. Nierenberg
Nierenberg Consulting Group

About the Author

Dr. Michael Lawrence Faulkner is the author or coauthor of 17 books. He is a professor at the Keller Graduate School of Management at DeVry University and a former U.S. Marine. Michael spent 30 years in a variety of leadership and executive management positions with Fortune 500 firms and major nonprofit trade associations. He also helped run the family business before beginning his second career in academics more than ten years ago. Michael is a Rotary International Fellow and a member of MENSA. He holds a Silver Certification by the Toastmasters International and has won the Keller Master Teacher Award and the Silver Apple Award by the NYC Direct Marketing Association. In addition to his Ph.D., Michael has earned two master's degrees, one from NYU, and an MBA from NYIT.

Preface

Why You Should Read This Book

Where am I going with this idea? Why the emphasis in the short run time frame—the thinking and approaches that will get you through your next speech or presentation?

First, I know from nearly 40 years of experience as a speaker, professor, and speaking coach that most people don't want to become great orators or memorable speakers; however, they do want to get through their next public speaking experience and feel like they did okay—even marginally better than they thought they could.

Second, I am confident that I can help you make this happen if you are willing to take just a couple hours to do three simple things:

1. Accept some basic fundamental truths about human nature and how this knowledge will help your presentation or speech.

2. Learn a few nonverbal communication signals—what they mean and how you can use them to enhance your presentation or speech.

3. Be willing to practice some simple steps that will support your next presentation or speech and make it better than average.

This book will help you realize that you can, without years of training, learn the techniques to help you become a good public speaker.

This book is not written to make you a great speaker or an eloquent rhetorical presenter. That requires a long process of learning, skill development, practice, and dedication that must take place over an extended period of time. But if you put in the effort to learn the easy rules identified in this book and commit to follow the simple guidelines, you will not only give a better presentation, but have the confidence to do it again and again. As a good speaker you can manage almost any speaking assignment required of you, and you will still be better than the vast majority of the presenters and speakers who have the gumption and desire to speak but not the training.

What This Book Is Not

This book is *not* intended to replace public speaking classes, presentation or communication courses, or any type of training and learning (formal or informal) regarding presenting, speaking, communicating, performing, debating, imparting, expounding, elocution, delivery, articulation, or vocalization.

This book is *not* intended to guide you through the various types of public speaking, (that is, informative, invitational, persuasive, invocative, debate, or small group speeches). Nor is it the traditional guide on how to give a speech. Hundreds of books, texts, videos, seminars, workshops, private coaches, teachers, Internet sites, and blogs do these things, and the intent of most of them is to turn you into a trained presenter, orator, or a gifted speaker. Unfortunately, as well-intended and professionally run as some of these are, I still believe this type of training has set up too many people for failure. This type of training typically uses the world's great speakers (for example, Lincoln, JFK, Reagan, Teddy Roosevelt, Churchill, Gandhi, FDR, Demosthenes, and Martin Luther King, Jr.) and great speeches as models to follow and emulate. The problem with this approach is most people won't be giving speeches of this nature at this level; they just want to get through their assigned or required presentation or speech and feel like they did a good job.

This book is written to help you get you through your next speaking gig with confidence, feeling good knowing you gave a solid presentation or speech. Timothy Koegel (2007), who wrote the *NY Times* best seller *The Exceptional Presenter*, said, "experience tells me that 80% of presenters are below average, 10% are average, 5% are good to very good, and 5% are exceptional."

He goes on to say that the percentage of presenters that can and should be able to give a good speech should be significantly higher, but most people never tap their full potential for several reasons, one being they don't have a system to develop the most basic skills.[1]

I wrote this book to help you learn the most basic skills of public speaking. This book arms you with the necessary skills to prepare you for your next presentation and for every presentation after that, so your audience is engaged and satisfied with your efforts.

Endnote

1. Koegel, Timothy. 2007. *The Exceptional Presenter.* Austin, TX: Greenleaf Book Group Press.

Introduction

In ancient mythology the gods condemned Sisyphus to ceaselessly rolling a rock to the top of a mountain only to have the rock roll back down due to its weight. This penalty was one in which effort and purpose are exerted toward accomplishing nothing. Sisyphus was doomed, but I saw the light. I spent nearly four decades pushing the rock uphill only to have it roll back down and having to repeat the process all over again. I am speaking of the attempt as a professor, consultant, and coach to turn unwilling students, clients, and workshop participants into excellent, top-notch public speakers. Then one day I had an epiphany and finally had to face reality.

It is simple. Most people hate the idea of standing up in front of other people and speaking. The data doesn't lie. Survey data shows people fear public speaking more than death. As unreasonable as it sounds, a significant number of people would actually prefer to be the person in the coffin rather than the person delivering the eulogy.

Most of us know intuitively or empirically the importance of communication skills. There is overwhelming evidence that it is one of the most important—if not *the* most important—life, job, and career skills we need. Still, schools, businesses, and individuals pay scant attention to improving this important skill. In most school curriculums, business training, and individual self-improvement programs, public speaking courses are still given relatively low priority. It isn't surprising when one stops to think about it. It's the same reason people often hesitate to take the necessary steps to improve their physical health—it requires hard work and continual effort.

Why do people hesitate to take the necessary steps to improve their communications skills? Why don't we work as hard to improve the one skill that would ensure greater career and personal success? The answer may be as simple as fear. The fear of public speaking, which we discuss in Chapter 2, "Step 2: The Fear of Public Speaking Is Real—Embrace It and Use It," is widespread, but manageable if understood. That is just one thing we attempt to do in this book: Help readers understand this fear and how to manage it.

There are no champions, no presidential czars, and no teacher unions pushing for a uniform syllabus or national test to measure improvement of individual presentation skills from year to year. There are no highly visible credible champions for the benefits of public speaking. So the individuals who understand the benefits and value how critical the skill is find the courses, locate the coaches, join the clubs such as Toastmasters International and Dale Carnegie, and otherwise discover ways to improve their verbal communication skills.

These people learn the skills and then reap the rewards. Other people who need more training and skill development live with the fear of speaking in front of others and avoid it until they are forced by circumstances to present. These situations can be traumatic and disabling. Many have the fear; it is what you do with the fear that counts.

Fifty thousand years ago, as hunter gatherers, we faced down furious beasts 50 times our size. We fought fearlessly against foes who threatened our families. We ate raw meat, slept under the stars, and struggled daily to survive. And survive we did. For hundreds of thousands of years *Homo sapiens* survived and evolved without language, without words.

Only after we discovered the technology of language did our species move out of our founding place in Africa and dominate the other human species in other parts of the world who were without language skills. We shared our experiences, our technology, and our culture, and for thousands of years before writing was discovered we shared this knowledge by telling simple stories to others.

Public speaking is telling stories to others.

1

Step 1: Think about Your Language and Keep It Simple

Language is archives of history.

—**Ralph Waldo Emerson**

Many people speak without clear intention; they simply blurt out whatever comes to mind. If you use the right words, speak with intention, and allow your mind and your actions to take on new purpose, you can speak with power and then act with power and influence. You can influence the lives of many people who listen to you. When you stand up before an audience of any size you have a unique opportunity and a significant leadership responsibility.

Communication is perhaps the most important human function in which we engage. Scientific evidence suggests that we don't trust our instincts driven by our *amygdala* (which some refer to as our animal brain). As much as we are capable, we have trouble absorbing nonverbal human communications adequately. We communicate verbally and nonverbally; however, if you think about it, we don't do it well. That might be because we aren't trained well or didn't listen to our teachers.

For the moment, forget about verbal communications and focus only on nonverbal communications or what we call body language. We know from empirical research that an overwhelming amount of human communications (as much as 97%) is conveyed by nonverbal cues.

Much of this body language is found in various facial expressions. Dr. Paul Ekman (1989) spent years studying facial cues and discovered 190 muscles in the nose and eye region of humans. Many of these muscles respond involuntarily and are keys to whether a person is telling the truth or lying. Ekman, professor emeritus in psychology at the University of California—San Francisco, is best known for furthering our understanding of nonverbal behavior, encompassing facial expressions and gestures. The American Psychological Association named Ekman one of the most influential psychologists of the twentieth century, and TIME Magazine (2009) hailed him as one of the 100 most influential people in the world (Paul Ekman Group, http://www.paulekman.com/paul-ekman).

Think about how our acculturation teaches us to deny our amygdala-driven instincts (such as, "We'll cross that bridge when we come to it"; "Don't judge a book by its cover"; "Don't jump to conclusions"; "Look before you leap"; "Act in haste, repent at your leisure"; "We should have a committee meeting to talk it over first"; and so on).

In spite of the knowledge of how much communication is transferred by nonverbal cues, our schools offer little education or training to improve human nonverbal perceptions. Instead, we are trained and encouraged by our upbringing and formal education to ignore or deny the existence of our intuition. We are told we must be practical, analytical, and thoughtful. All this has simply led us to ignore how the vast amount of communication actually takes place—through nonverbal communications.

Research by Dr. Ekman, his associate Wallace V. Friesen, and others has shown that in spite of wide cultural differences in language and cultural norms, 11 facial nonverbal expressions are recognized around the world. In the 1990s, Dr. Ekman proposed a list of these basic emotions, including a range of positive and negative emotions that are not all encoded in facial muscles.

The emotions are amusement, contempt, contentment, embarrassment, excitement, guilt, pride in achievement, relief, satisfaction, sensory pleasure, and shame (Ekman, 1989, 143-164).

Some of the muscle movements described by Dr. Ekman are so subtle that only a trained expert can detect movement. However, most of these facial muscle movements and especially the subtle ones can actually be observed and felt by the amygdala of people even if these people did not consciously perceive the movement. The amygdala is the almond shaped organ of the brain or what some refer to as the animal or reptile brain. Long before humans developed our thinking brain—the cerebral cortex—our amygdala functioned as our emotional radar and provided the fight-or-flight emotion.

Fortunately for our species, we chose flight early on in a hostile environment where we were outgunned by bigger, faster, and fiercer predators. We were low on the food chain, but we had the advantage of having the amygdala, which allowed our species the time to survive and evolve.

MOST HUMAN COMMUNICATION IS NONVERBAL

We know from research that the vast majority of communication from one human to another, from a speaker to the audience, and from the audience to the speaker is nonverbal. One of the most frequently quoted statistics on nonverbal communication is that 93% of all daily communication is nonverbal. Various media channels, outlets, professors, and popular books frequently quote this specific number, which is attributed to Professor Albert Mehrabian (1981) of UCLA, who conducted several studies in the 1970s of nonverbal communications and came up with the formula that only 7% of human communication is actually conducted through verbal language. Thus the resulting calculation that 93% of all human communication is nonverbal. Other research in this area has shown different results from Dr. Mehrabian's. Whether the actual percentage of nonverbal communication is 97% or 90% or 80% or 60% isn't the most important thing. What really matters is nonverbal communications are significant and the most crucial aspect of human communications, and we simply cannot ignore them.

With this knowledge we can begin to grasp the strategy of how the speech or presentation will go. Experience tells us that if a speaker makes communication simple, the audience will appreciate this and respond more favorably than if they have to work and struggle to look for hidden meanings and undertones.

We know that man communicated with other men for thousands of years prior to the invention of human language. Long before human verbal language, people found mates, raised families, hunted together, joined in early tribal communities, and selected leaders, and yet there was virtually no innovation, hardly any art or crafts, no real trade or commerce, and a relatively short life span. Then along came language, and everything changed.

Your speech or presentation begins with your audience making what we refer to as a micro snap judgment of you even before you utter a sound. This is called by many the first impression.

The first impression starts the moment you appear by standing up or walking to the speaking spot (podium, position from which you will make your speech or presentation). This initial or first impression is critical for two reasons. First, it is critical because so much of the audience's opinion of you and what you are about to say is going to take place in micro seconds. Each audience member's amygdala is registering an instant opinion of you (and you have not yet said a word). The second reason it is important is you have almost total control over this initial impression. We cover this in greater detail in later chapters, but the way you are dressed and groomed, the way you carry yourself, and the manner in which you show your poise and grace as you walk to the spot to where you deliver your speech or presentation, gives you great influence over this first impression.

Think Simple

The first step to getting through your next speech or presentation is to STOP! Take a breath and begin to think this through as a simple plan. Simple doesn't necessarily mean easy. It means it does not have to consume you. All important activities and endeavors should begin with planning, and written plans are the best. I am not suggesting a speaker or presenter should begin with a formal Microsoft Office Business Plan template. Many successful enterprises and innovations began life on the back of an envelope or, like the ubiquitous ATM machine, on the corner of an envelope. The first step, however, should be to plan out the strategy and the next steps and write them down or type them out.

Committing a plan to paper provides one with the opportunity to create simple, clear action steps. The simpler the thinking the easier it is to adjust when changes need to be made.

Your plan, like most plans, will probably not face a smooth path, but forming it and writing it down makes it a commitment you can carry through with regardless of the obstacles. Most people, and this includes business owners, don't write down even the simplest of business plans. The two most frequently given reasons:

1. No time to do it.

2. Don't know how to write one.

Committing to the simplest of plans eliminates the excuse of no time. A simple plan should take no more than 20 minutes.

Another benefit of keeping the thinking simple is most answers to the problems we encounter and most solutions to the problems we face are the simplest answers and solutions rather than the complex ones we so often think will be best. In academics we often make reference to Ockham's Razor. In a great over simplification it means the simplest explanation is usually the right one.

The next excuse, not knowing how, is eliminated by the following simple template.

The Simple Plan Components

All plans differ in their content but to provide a general format, here are some suggested contents:

1. Goal—What is it you want to accomplish?

2. Objectives/tactics—What actual steps do *you* have to take to make this goal happen? What actual steps do others have to take to make this goal happen? Who are these people and what will you have to do to inform them of their roles and responsibilities?

3. What is the time line for this goal? What is the time line for the objectives and tactics? By when will these things be accomplished?

4. What obstacles stand in the way? How can these obstacles be overcome? What help do you need in doing this?

Start with Things You Can Control— Dress Simply

My advice to speakers and presenters is to dress simply. This does not mean you should dress in a casual or sloppy manner. It means you should dress in business attire or appropriate attire for the occasion (casual for resort setting, formal for ceremony, and so on). You can be elegant and fashionable but *do not overdress*. Flashy attire or an extraordinary appearance creates an image of someone trying to impress or going overboard, which can lead to a less than favorable initial impression. The best rule is dress similarly to the majority of your audience.

For men, a necktie is critical. A man can wear an off-the-rack inexpensive suit and make it work with a crisp clean white or light blue shirt and a tie. Wearing a tie with absolute confidence will translate at the first moment's glance, respect will be established. The tie is the first thing people notice, and if it is sharp, expensive looking, stylish, and tied correctly, a man will make a strong first impression. People seeing a man wearing a great tie make the assumption he must be a professional regardless of his age. Something many men don't realize is the properly selected and worn tie can serve to help correct some physical characteristics. A very tall man might want to wear ties with horizontal patterns, whereas a more stout man might want to wear ties that have vertical patterns. Narrow ties help accentuate a man's stature. A man's vertical dimensions are equally important.

Taller men receive benefits from a slightly longer tie that accentuates a positive height. Shorter men can generate the appearance of additional height by having a slightly blunted tie style. In the end, a man should seek to have precise personal clothing measurements. However, undetected adjustments can be made and these can provide subtle aids that enhance a man's confidence.

Don't forget your shoes. Since your speech or presentation will be done from a standing position it is wise to wear comfortable shoes. While you may be inclined to buy an appropriate new outfit for your speech or presentation, I would advise wearing footwear that you have broken in.

It is always a good idea to get information about your audience in advance, and part of this information is how they will be dressed. As a speaker you should match your audience's attire as well as language.

Women can often have a more difficult time than men when it comes to determining how to follow the "dress simple" advice for public speaking. Without getting into the reasons or the fairness, society just imposes far more rules and restraints on women's attire than men's. Rather than using the speaking engagement to make a political or social statement, women speakers have to recognize that they have a more difficult task in their clothing choices. In most cases, pant suits; slacks and blouses; dresses and skirts; and dressier tops are appropriate. The same clothing that would be worn to a business office or business event is appropriate. And, the same rule applies—don't over or under dress for your audience.

I would advise keeping jewelry and accessories to a minimum. You will be in front of people and you want their attention on you and what you are saying, not on flashy watches, necklaces, scarves, pins, or chains. Another thing you should remember is to remove your attendee or speaker's badge before you stand up to speak. It is just another distraction you don't need.

One last word on cultural attire: If you are speaking to a group that is closely tied to their native culture, your topic is about this culture, and you are genetically part of this culture, it is appropriate to wear attire from this culture for your speech or presentation. Otherwise, avoid dressing, speaking, or acting as if you are a part of the culture, making a faux attempt to pretend you are something you are not. It is phony, unprofessional, and potentially offensive to your audience.

THE TECHNOLOGY OF LANGUAGE

Kevin Kelly's (2010) *What Technology Wants* is a provocative book that introduces a brand new view of technology in which he suggests that technology is not just hardwired metal and chips, but a living, natural system whose origin goes back to the Big Bang. My intention is not to review the book; however, I do recommend every manager, supervisor, boss, mentor, coach, influencer, instigator, team leader, team member, entrepreneur, capitalist, investor, futurist, provocateur, teacher, professor, minister, government employee, politician, or new parent read it. One point of Kelly's book that I refer to often is the technology of language.

We know humans developed language about 50,000 years ago. Kelly traces the development of human language to the behavior of humans. By tracing the behavior of the human species we can follow Kelly's argument that language followed certain human behavior patterns. At some point about 2.5 million years ago, the human brain grew larger and we began to use more refined tools than our ape line. Archaeological evidence shows the growth of human brains and simple stone tools. At this point, the first migration began out of Africa for two human species: the *Neanderthal* to Europe and the *Homo Erectus* to Asia. *Homo Sapiens* remained in Africa.

It is important to note that all three species had the same brain size and same rough tools. Over the next 50 million years, all three species developed at about the same pace (none with language skills). All three species hunted with simple tools, developed crude art, had children, lived relatively short lives, did not bury their dead, and the population of these groups remained unchanged. The period for these species is known as the Mesolithic Period. Around 50,000 years ago, something radical happened.

The *Homo Sapiens* in Africa suddenly underwent significant genetic changes. They became full of ideas and innovations and developed the desire to innovate, move, and explore new worlds. They spread out of Africa in what is known as the second migration, and in 40,000 years settled in every corner of the earth. In a fraction of one percent of the time it took for the first migration to take place and for the first wave to settle in one spot, the *Homo Sapiens* covered the world.

Not only did they have the desire to move, but they were also full of innovation. They developed fish hooks, fish nets, various sized spears, bows, and arrows; they started to sew; they used hearth stoves; they buried their dead; and they created sophisticated art and jewelry. *Homo Sapiens* developed trade, pottery, animal traps, and built garbage pits. In the process of mastering these innovative things, they overwhelmed their *Neanderthal* and *Homo Erectus* brothers, making *Homo Sapiens* the only human species on the planet.

The question we have to ask is what caused this radical change in *Homo Sapiens*? How did it occur? Some argue that a point mutation or a rewiring of the brain caused it. We are not proposing a cause; we simply state the fact that there was an outcome from what radically changed and that something different occurred 50,000 years ago. That radical change was that language occurred, changing mankind forever.

The special significance of language as a great idea lies in the fact that it is related to all other great ideas, insofar as ideas and thoughts are expressed to other persons, for the most part, in words, in speech, and in language.

Today, we seem to view language as an enemy, a barrier to communication, and a tyranny of words. There is even a debate about whether communication and speech are the same thing.

The Power of Words

> *Words are, of course, the most powerful drug used by mankind.*

> **—Rudyard Kipling**

Dr. Frank Luntz (2007) said, "You can have the best message in the world, but the person on the receiving end will always understand it through the prism of his or her own emotions, preconceptions, prejudices, and preexisting beliefs. It's not enough to be correct or reasonable or even brilliant. The key to successful communication is to take an imaginative leap of stuffing yourself right into your listener's shoes to know what they are thinking and feeling in the deepest recesses of their mind and heart."

Once you have spoken words, they are no longer yours. Other people filter them, translate them, evaluate them, and measure them through their biases, life experiences, prejudices, and world views. Words create impressions, images, and expectations. They build psychological connections between the speaker and listener.

They influence how we think. Words impose in the speaker an extra special responsibility. The speaker/writer must choose words carefully to make them appropriate for the situation.

Words have the power to affect both the physical and emotional health of people to whom we speak, for better and worse. Words used to influence are inspiring, uplifting, challenging, encouraging, motivating, and persuading. They can be visionary, they can change people's lives for the better. Words coupled with the use of power, coercion, force, and deception, don't just have a brief or short-term impact.

Their influence, good or bad, can last a lifetime. Verbal communication is a powerful human instrument, and we must learn to use it properly. We need to not only learn to think about speaking in new ways, but we need to learn to think about language, words, and human nature, psychology, and sociology. They are interconnected.

At the end of World War II, the Allied Powers sent a message to the Japanese demanding surrender. The Japanese responded with the word "mokusatsu," which translates as either "to ignore" or "to withhold comment." The Japanese meant that they wished to withhold comment, to discuss, and then decide. The Allies translated mokusatsu as the Japanese deciding to ignore the demand for surrender. The Allies ended the war by dropping the bomb and transforming the world we live in forever. The effect that words can have is incredible: to inform, persuade, inflict hurt, ease pain, end war or start one, and kill thousands or even millions of people. They can get your point across or destroy any hope of your idea ever being understood.

Poorly chosen words or speech used for personal hubris or evil can impact self-esteem, destroy morale, kill enthusiasm, inflame bias, incite hatred, lower expectations, and hold people back. They can even make people physically or mentally ill. Inappropriate words can make work and home toxic and abusive environments.

Many empirical studies show that people who live and/or work in toxic environments suffer more colds, more cases of flu, more heart attacks, more depression, more of almost all chronic disorders, physical and emotional, than people who report living or working in happy, enjoyable, caring environments. The old adage, "Sticks and stones can break your bones, but words can never hurt you" is simply bad advice.

Verbal insults and verbal abuse can affect your emotions and behavior. This is well documented in science. For example, scientists have found that just hearing sentences about senior citizens led sample subjects to walk more slowly. In other studies, researchers have observed that when students are given standardized tests and told the tests are "intelligence exams," the average scores are from 10% to 20% lower than results from the same exam given to similar students who are told it is "just an exam." In still other research, individuals who read words of "loving kindness" showed increases in self-compassion, improved mood, and reduced anxiety. There is information about the medicinal benefits of power verbs as well as a warning about the power of words, which, if used inappropriately, can actually make individuals physically ill.

In the study, published in *Pain*, researchers used functional magnetic resonance tomography (fMRI) to examine how 16 healthy people processed words associated with experiencing pain. The brain scans revealed which parts of the brain activate in response to hearing words. In the first experiment, researchers asked the participants to imagine situations that correspond with words associated with pain, such as "excruciating," "paralyzing," and "grueling." Researchers also asked participants to imagine situations that correspond with negative words that aren't painful, such as "dirty" and "disgusting."

Finally, researchers also had participants respond to neutral and positive words. In the second experiment, the participants read the same words, but they were distracted by a brainteaser. The results showed that in both cases there is a clear response in the brain's pain-processing centers with the words associated with pain, but there is no such activity pattern in response to the other words.

The authors of the study say preserving painful experiences as memories in the brain might be an evolutionary response to allow humans to avoid painful situations that might be dangerous (Warner 2015).

On the other hand, well-chosen words or speech, for the benefit of good or hope, can motivate or inspire others to greater feats and deeds. They can offer hope, create vision, and impact thinking, beliefs, and the behaviors of others. Positive words can alter the results of strategies, plans, objectives, and even people's lives. Positive words can uplift and encourage people and set them on a goal or path they otherwise might never have thought possible.

Power verbs express an action that is to be taken or that has been taken. A powerful verb, when used correctly, has the power to impact your life whether you are going into battle, running for president, or simply interviewing for a job.

We know that words create impressions, ideas, images, concepts, and facsimiles. Therefore, the words that we hear and read influence how we think and consequently how we behave. This means there is a correlation between the words we select and use and the results that occur. Using powerful verbal imagery helps people imagine vivid images and helps them figuratively and literally see the concepts mentioned. This was first discovered in the early twentieth century and was initially known as the *Perky Effect*; it was later called *visual simulation*. Individuals can project abstract thoughts. Almost everyone does this from time to time, but we refer to it as day dreaming.

When you day dream, you are completely awake and the eyes are wide open, yet you imagine being somewhere else, doing something else. Visual simulation impacts what people hear and how fast they respond. Cognitive psychologist Rolf Zwann has done a lot of research on the topic of how people describe objects and shapes to which they are exposed. His experiment includes showing people visuals and asking for responses and then providing audio prompts before the visual stimulation.

People are asked to describe the objects. Particularly if the subjects are prompted with words or sentences with the object beforehand, the results indicate that people respond faster because what they see and hear is mentally simulated beforehand (Bergen, 95). Many studies have confirmed that people construct visual simulations of objects they hear or read about.

People construct shape and orientation simulation. Studies show that when people listen they more often look at the set of objects that fit with the meaning of the verb, even before they hear the name of the relevant object. People make predictions about what the rest of the sentence contains as soon as words that they have already heard start to constrain what could reasonably follow. People start to cobble their understanding of the sentence incrementally (Bergen, 125).

Grammar helps get the visual simulation going by pulling together all the pieces contributed by the words in the correct configuration. People more easily and clearly comprehend your meaning if you have structured your sentence correctly. One particular form is the transitive sentence. It has a transfer of possession meaning. Transitive sentences start with a noun or noun phrase, are followed by a verb, and then have one or two noun phrases. The following is an example:

> The outgoing CEO kicked the problem down the road to the new CEO.

If we use the intended transfer definition, the transitive sentence describes an intended transfer of an object to a recipient, and naturally the recipient must be capable of receiving something (Bergen, 106). Words we use can even be impacted by our background and other influences.

Consider the words buy and invest. If you are selling life insurance, you want the customer to buy, but in your mind the purchase is a long-term investment. The premiums get invested, the face value of the policy grows, there is eventually a loan value, and the investment appreciates beyond the purchase price. However the customer thinks in terms of buying and how much it costs. The issue comes full circle again if the customer does buy and if he wants the insurance company to make good investments.

Nan Russell, President of Mountain Works Communications, an employee training firm, introduces this word choice: problem or challenge. Would you rather your boss see your mistake as a problem or a challenge? Is it just semantics? Problems are things that need to be fixed; challenges are met. Different words evoke a different set of emotions and feelings. People usually have a much more positive feeling about "meeting a challenge" than "fixing a problem."

ON WORDS

Words affect who we are. Without words, we would be isolated. Language and its nuances are uniquely human. Language is something we learn completely by audio cues—in other words, by listening. We do this because human brains are hardwired—genetically wired—to learn language by listening as an infant. It is interesting that we are not even consciously aware we are cognitively learning.

Before we had the ability to speak words, others could understand us. Our species survived and advanced, making other members understand with nonverbal cues. For millions of years, children communicated to their mothers that they were hungry. Men communicated to women and women to men that they were interested in them as partners. Hunters collaborated on big animal kills long before a word was spoken; man even showed others how to start and keep a fire going long before there were words for such things. Anthropologists believe the spoken word appeared on the scene around 50,000 B.C. Humans used grunts, pointing, and body language for a long time.

Using Words in Special Ways

We know that more than 97% of human communication involves nonverbal cues (body language). To have a successful presentation, speech, or presidential debate performance, we must compose a sophisticated but seamless message, uniting our words in the proper rhythm, and use the corresponding nonverbal cues. If the words chosen do not match the nonverbal cues or vice versa the audience might get confused and the message might be diminished, or worse, ignored.

In the world of movies, theater, art, and entertainment, words have a dramatic impact. In a recent *Wall Street Journal* edition, a special report titled "What's In a Name?" discussed a number of box office successes that might have a different result if their original titles had not been changed.

For example, The Bogart classic *Casablanca* had an original title *Everybody Comes to Ricks*. The Julia Roberts/Richard Gere blockbuster *Pretty Woman* had the original title *$3,000*. The successful *G.I. Jane* was supposed to be released as *In Defense of Honor*. The world might not have ever remembered Diane Keaton and Woody Allen in *Anhedonia*, which was fortunately changed to *Annie Hall* (*Wall Street Journal*, Arena, October 19, 2012, p. D1).

Throughout history, many memorable quotes have demonstrated how what is said is just as important as how it is said. For example, there is an old story that went around Washington, D.C., about Lyndon B. Johnson when he was stumping for state political office, he was surpassingly debating an opponent and was asked the difference between himself and the opposing candidate. He allegedly replied, "He matriculated and I never matriculated."

Some of the most famous speeches made by Abraham Lincoln are memorable not just for the message, but for the fact that he condensed an enormous amount of information into them. It was not only the power of his words, but also his cadence that made the impact of the speeches more powerful. His second inaugural speech was only 700 words, and the *Gettysburg Address* was just under 3 minutes long. But Lincoln understood that he could make his simple words more powerful by altering the rate at which he delivered those words, the volume changes during the speech, the differences in pitch and tone (whether he spoke in a low deeper voice of wisdom or a higher trailing off voice of authority and the occasional injection of silence or what we call an intentional pause).

It really comes down to a simple rule—*Keep it simple.* The fact is most audiences have short attention spans—for many reasons—and you need to cater to this.

Paint pictures with your words. The audience needs to be able to hear what you are thinking.

The human brain thinks in a sequence of images that complete a thought and that can be shared as a story, example, case, formula, or in other descriptive ways. If your presentation goal is to describe how to create a beautifully decorated birthday cake, the approach should be a step-by-step linear link to the finished cake. For example, you could begin by discussing the eggs used, how much flour is needed, and how they are blended together. You could then discuss how the butter and baking powder are blended in with the mixture, the batter is poured into a pan, and then the pan placed in the oven. Once the cake is finished baking it is cooled and then decorated with icing.

If you mention a birthday cake most humans simply see the end result of a decorated birthday cake, so trying to tell an audience just the end result of anything without sharing the building blocks or sequence of steps in a story leaves them cold.

This approach works for any topic or idea. Speakers need to tell their audience a story about the topic by dividing the topic into pieces or segments culminating in the finished or completed topic.

WHAT IS THE SPECIAL SIGNIFICANCE OF LANGUAGE?

Language accelerates learning; it speeds up innovation by permitting communication and coordination. A new idea can spread quickly if someone can explain it and communicate it to others before they have to discover it themselves. We use language, verbal and nonverbal, to make sense of our world. We use it to interact and to confirm, beg, act, command, inquire, network, court, teach, coach, and entertain. A few verbal and nonverbal messages can influence us, change our minds, cause us do something different, and change our position or vote.

Limit the Number of Key Points

Studies show that around 25% of audiences of all types can only remember between two to three key points of a 50-minute talk within an hour of the event. Recall erodes even worse and more quickly over the next 24 hours.

Attention span and recall issues lead us to the point that speakers and presenters who are the most memorable are those who zero in on fewer—not more—key points. Memorable speakers also tell simple stories, case studies, and examples and offer proof points highlighting fewer key points. Audiences for speeches and presentations do not want to be challenged. They want to hear something interesting and preferably something that has to do with the speaker.

How to Speak Extemporaneously and Make a Toast

My emphasis on simplicity now provides you with the ability to be called on to speak extemporaneously (even if for just a minute or two) and be asked to give a toast either on the spur of the moment or with advance notice. If you can focus on the idea that simplicity in thought and follow-through will help you manage either or both of these situations, you can meet either with more confidence than you ever thought. Let's look at the situations.

Speaking Extemporaneously

First, the extemporaneous event. It could happen when you least expect it, which means people fear it most because they have no time to think or prepare or organize their thoughts. Of course everyone in the room is in the exact same position. However, I have a simple solution that if you learn and practice once or twice you could be the one person in the audience, who if called upon, will look like a polished professional speaker, and the rest of the crowd will sit there in awe.

Here is the simple solution. In any extemporaneous situation the person asking you to comment or to make a remark is using a technique of "audience involvement." There are several reasons why a speaker would include the audience:

- The speaker is looking for people to confirm and endorse his ideas. In terms of audience participation this is sometimes called "spectating." In other words you are supposed to just agree with the speaker.

  It is completely up to you whether you go along and agree with the speaker's point of view or choose your own position. Either choice has consequences, so you need to be prepared for each. The speaker is in control and depending on her style can make you look small or like a significant part of the event.

- The speaker is looking for people to provide "enhanced engagement" to enrich his program that has just been delivered. The format involves the speaker moving to the audience and keeping control of the microphone. The speaker is looking for a quick creative idea or thought and generally only allows seconds for an audience member to get involved. These speakers are looking for approval and confirmation of their ideas.

- The speaker is using the audience to "crowdsource" or troll for enhanced content to improve the program. This is a good opportunity to be as open and expressive as you wish.

- The speaker is showing off and is trying to demonstrate her excellent skills with an amateur, trying to draw the audience member into the presentation, which of course, the speaker still controls.

- The speaker has finished early and needs to use up time.

Whatever the reason, it doesn't matter to you if you have a microphone stuck in your face and have been asked to comment, give your opinion, or ask a question. At this moment the rest of the entire audience is breathing a sigh of relief that they were not asked. This makes them a friendly audience, and they are all rooting for you.

If you have been following the program contents, you should have some idea of your own opinion, feelings, world view, or beliefs on the topic.

If called upon to make impromptu remarks, be ready to express these. This will help you know you have something worthwhile to say.

There is a rule of improvisational art, and it is never reject the premise. Accept what has been handed to you and work with it. Rejecting, resisting, overtly attempting to change the topic or subject only makes the situation more confusing and unsettling. Your resistance can make you look small, accepting makes you look professional and in control.

Here are the simple steps for the next one to two minutes (which may sound like a long time but in reality is a short time span).

1. Stand and accept the microphone smiling all the time (don't resist, shake your head, or hold up your hands). The speaker standing over you has a commanding position, and you can only look bad sitting and trying to hold off a request.

2. Thank the speaker for the opportunity to say a few words to the wonderful people in attendance today, move slightly away from the speaker. (You are choosing your own speaking space; it shows strength.) Keep smiling.

3. Look out into the audience (not at the speaker). Keep smiling.

4. There are a number of models you can use on which to build a one- to two- minute response to any question or comment concerning politics, economics, social issues, education, business, family, religion, philosophy, physics, money, immigration, taxation, sports, music, social media, or any other topic.

Pick something, anything that you can use as a *sequential memory device* to help you organize your thoughts. And don't just think of the object, visualize it as well. Here are some examples:

- **Colors**—Red, yellow, green (red=stop, yellow=slow, green = go). For example, visualize a stop light traffic signal and select the colors.

- **Geometric designs**—Box, circle, triangle (box=even sides but no easy exits; circle=smooth sides, easy access; triangle=strong base, difficult assent; see Figure 1.1).

Figure 1.1 Memory aid: Divide your subject or thoughts into threes or triads

- **Seasons**—Summer, winter, fall.

- **Distance**—Far off, middle, nearby.

- **Numbers**—Fractions, single digits, multiple numbers.

- **Heights**—Low, medium, high.

- **The room you're in**—Back, middle, front, or the floor, tables, ceiling.

The options are nearly endless. You can select anything that comes to your mind from your past experience or whatever you feel most comfortable with. The point is to have in your repertoire one or two models that use the sequence formula that you have practiced several times. Then when the time comes that you're called upon to make extemporaneous comments or remarks you perform like a pro.

A quick scenario will help. Let's say you are in an audience where the speaker has been discussing his views on the negative impact of the loss of traffic ticket revenue earmarked for local public schools from digital traffic cameras that have been recently removed as a result of significant consumer complaints.

The speaker makes a claim that the community position has harmed the future of the children and puts the microphone in front of you asking for your opinion.

Following the "be simple" model, you stand smiling, take the microphone, and step away from the speaker looking into the audience.

Assume for this scenario that you disagree with the speaker's position. You thank the speaker for the opportunity to comment:

> "Thank you Ms. _____ for the opportunity to comment on this important issue. We all feel it is important, which is why we are here today. [15 seconds have already elapsed.]
>
> Like many issues we must face, this one has different perspectives and shapes and those are like geometric shapes.
>
> **Some points are like a box,** many sided; some arguments appear to be strong but when examined closely they are quite contained and difficult to escape into the full light to be examined. We need to spend more time turning these around and around looking at the edges and sides, top and bottom. It is like solving Rubik's cube—very difficult. It can be done, but it's not easy. It requires more time.
>
> **Other points are like circles;** they seem smooth and well thought out, easy to access. All the arguments for and against seem to have equal opportunity for all to see so the proper decision can be made.
>
> **Other points are like triangles;** there appears to be a firm base, solid and established evidence for one point of view. However, as time goes on evidence and information seems to cause less and less support until eventually there is very little support at the point where the decision has to be made.

It appears to me as though the community has seen this decision as a triangle, and this is where we are—at the point."

[Depending on how many pauses you put in, nearly 1:30 seconds have elapsed.]

Here is a scenario using color:

"The question we are dealing with has many subtle variations like a color palette. On one hand, the darker shades of red (metaphor/simile) are those that need more light shed on them to help us see the answers. On the other hand, the lighter more colorful shades of the issue such as yellow seem clear and direct. Unfortunately, like a painter's palette the issues we must deal with have many shades and many subtleties that require our concerted thought leadership. Real leaders, however, see green and just go toward solutions and answers.

Of course, any short quote or saying is a great way to begin or end.

Oh yes, the final step: Hand the microphone back to the speaker (whose mouth will be hanging open in amazement) and sit down with a coy smile. If you want to add a slight flair drop the microphone on the table and sit.

Making a Toast Extemporaneously

If you're invited to give a toast extemporaneously, consider it an honor. The host believes you, over all the other guests, are the most talented, gifted, or gracious and should have the honor. So, rather than feel put upon or resentful, you should feel proud to have been selected.

Unlike a member of an audience in which a speaker has asked for a comment, a request for you to give a toast provides you a little more time to gather a few thoughts and think of your theme.

These are the steps to make a successful and memorable toast:

- Accept the invitation graciously.

- Smile.

- Keep it simple.

- Use the same sequential memory technique as described previously to help you organize your thoughts.

- Example: "I've known [the honoree] for a long time and as time passes like seasons, memories of [the honoree] have different impacts. I remember meeting the [the honoree] in the spring of our careers. Our careers and jobs were in bloom and [honoree's] life was in full blossom. I had the pleasure to watch [honoree's] life and career move into full summer where he/she had great success and grew as a person and professional. Now in the winter of his/her life he/she is not planning on hibernating but looking forward to the next spring and making new goals. Here is to those endeavors."

- Keep it short. The best toast is less than 3 minutes; 1 minute is the best.

- Make sure to mention the honoree's name, but do not look at him or her until the toast is complete.

- Do not offer embarrassing, private, or secret information about the honoree.

- *Do not clink glasses with the honoree* (unless the toast is in a beer garden or bar).

Making a Toast with Advance Notice

If you are asked to give a toast and are given advance notice, all the same advice mentioned previously applies. However, you have the advantage of preparing the remarks in advance, and you have the opportunity to rehearse, so you do not have to use notes. There is nothing worse than someone standing up to toast his "lifelong, very best friend in the world" with feeling and passion and pulling out note cards or sheets of paper to tell the audience how important this person is to him!

A toast is an honor; it is moment to salute an honoree not embarrasses or humiliate him. It certainly is not the time to drag out the moment and make the entire assemblage feel awkward. Whoever started the long-winded dragged out story after story form of toasting did no one any favors. This form of toasting is humiliating, debasing, and counter to what a toast is supposed to do.

So perform a toast as it was originally designed to be: an honor to some-one—brief, succinct, and dignified. The person making the toast should at all costs avoid these things, which are serious gaffes:

1. Talking about yourself other than in reference to how you know the honoree.

2. Talking too long; a toast should last no longer than 2 minutes.

3. Using cliché passé phrases (the guests have heard them all many times before)

Setting Up the Toast

The toaster should make sure the wine glasses are full and that his glass is sparking clean. The toast is most likely to be given under bright lights, and the toaster does not want his glass to be dirty or cloudy.

The toaster needs to make sure the honoree is present.

The toaster needs to get the attention of the guests. This could take a minute or so.

The Body Language of the Toaster

1. Stand up straight. (Shoulders level to floor)

2. Smile.

3. Act confidently.

4. Don't raise or lower your head. (This affects your vocal cords.)

5. Make eye contact as you look around the room.

6. Maintain eye contact with attendees.

7. Hold your glass at waist height.

8. Do not gesture with your glass.

9. Raise your glass to eye level at the end of your toast in the direction of the honoree.

10. The toaster may be the first person to drink.

11. When you are toasting in a formal setting, don't clink glasses.

Key Takeaways

- Dress simply and look like your audience. You want to feel as physically comfortable as possible.

- Keep your talk simple. Use shorter more impactful words familiar to the audience. Speak their language.

- Make fewer points for the audience to remember (two or three are optimal). Most people do not have the capacity to remember more than three points so why present more than they are capable of remembering?

- When you are going to make a key point to the audience, tell them what you are going to do. It is perfectly fine to say "This is a key point."

- Paint pictures with your simple language. Successful radio announcers are capable of getting audiences to listen to someone they can't see by the announcer's ability to use words to paint a picture the audience can imagine. Paint pictures with your thoughts and ideas and words.

- Use stories, case studies, and examples to make your points (preferably contemporary ones and things that are familiar to your audience).

- Most audiences prefer to hear some stories about you, the speaker.

- Use power verbs instead of dull verbs. Make your sentences come alive. Power verbs are full of action and force. They make your words more dynamic and help you speak with passion.

- Smile when you speak.

- Speak slowly unless you intend to speed up for emphasis. Changing your pace is okay. Pausing is a powerful speaking tool; it generates tension, interest, and anticipation in your audience.

- Raising or lowering your head stretches or constricts your vocal cords and makes your voice pitch different (changes the pitch from a higher to a lower pitch). Knowing this allows you to control your pitch.

- If you are going give a toast, make it dignified and brief.

Chapter 1 Notes

Bergen, Benjamin. 2007. Experimental Methods for Simulation Semantics. In *Methods of Cognitive Linguistics,* ed. Monica Irene Gonzalez-Marquez, Seana Coulson Mittelberg, and Michael J. Spivey, 277, 302. Philadelphia: John Benjamin's Company.

Ekman, Paul. 1989. The Argument and Evidence about Universals in Facial Expression of Emotion. In *Handbook of Social Psychophysiology*, ed. H. Wagner and A. Manstead, 143-164. Chichester: John Wiley & Sons.

Essays of Ralph Waldo Emerson, The. 1987. Ferguson, Alfred Riggs, and Jean Ferguson Carr, Eds., 13. Boston: Harvard University Press.

Kelly, Kevin. 2010. *What Technology Wants.* New York: Viking Press.

Luntz, Frank. 2007. *Words That Work: It's Not What You Say That Counts, It's What People Hear.* New York: Hyperion Books.

Mehrabian, Albert. 1981. *Silent Messages: Implicit Communication of Emotions and Attitudes.* Belmont, CA: Wadsworth, 75-80.

Warner, Jennifer. Words Really Do Hurt. WebMD Health News, http://www.webmd.com/pain-management/news/20100402/words-really-do-hurt. Accessed, February 6, 2015.

2

Step 2: The Fear of Public Speaking Is Real—Embrace It and Use It

Our doubts are traitors,

And make us lose the good we oft might win

By fearing to attempt.

—William Shakespeare

Let's come right out and take this on. The fear of public speaking is real for many people. It's common; so if it is something you've experienced, recognize that it is nearly universal. The so-called experts who try to help by clinically discussing it as irrational or rational with their accompanying data, cures, or workarounds don't make it any better. Does it make you feel better knowing that other people—including this author—experience performance anxiety? I didn't think so. Many experienced speakers and performers still have some form of performance or speaker anxiety. There is no secret cure, only the individual's desire to channel the nervous energy and instead of it working against you, make it work for you in the form of a passionate delivery.

Everyone has a worst fear, or two, or more. While experts tell us human beings are born with only two natural fears—the fear of falling and the fear of loud noises—we are acculturated and learn from society to be fearful of other things, such as ill health, flying, being poor, loss of love, old age, dying, and, of course, the thought of or the act of standing up and speaking or performing in front of a group of people. The layman's term for this fear is *stage fright.*

Other terms are sometimes interchanged that are all in the same family of fears. I am not interested in specific diagnoses or medical definitions, other than that the first two mentioned are debilitating and the last three are common. Most people who experience the last three fears in this list manage them successfully:

- **Panic attack**—A panic attack is a sudden period of intense fear or discomfort accompanied by a number of symptoms. The fear builds to a peak rapidly in a few minutes and is often accompanied by a sense of imminent danger or impending doom and an urge to escape.

- **Social phobia**—This is a marked and persistent fear of social or performance situations in which the individual feels certain that embarrassment may occur. People can only be diagnosed if their avoidance, fear, or anxious anticipation of encountering the social or performance situation interferes significantly with the person's daily routine, occupational functioning, or social life, or if the person is markedly distressed about having the phobia. In feared social or performance situations, individuals with social phobia experience concerns about embarrassment and are afraid that others will judge them to be anxious, weak, crazy, or stupid. The person with social phobia typically avoids the feared situation.

- **Trait anxiety**—This is a generalized disposition to feel threatened by a wide range of nonharmful conditions. Persons who are high in trait anxiety tend to be anxious in many situations.

- **State anxiety**—This condition is situational and is related to specific environmental situations such as public speaking, musical performance, job interviews, spiders, snakes, flying in an airplane, shooting free throw baskets, throwing a baseball, or taking a test. One's feelings of apprehension are focused and localized. Situational anxiety such as this can be managed by specific behavioral strategies.

- **Performance anxiety**—This is a state of anxiety or stage fright prior to and/or during a performance.

Fear of public speaking is reportedly the *number one* fear of American adults, with a significant number of people reporting in surveys that they fear speaking in public more than death. What does this say about us that we would rather be the person in the coffin than the person delivering the eulogy? It says some people experience a tremendous amount of pain and suffering because of a fear.

If this fear isn't treated or managed it can take a huge toll on people as it erodes their effectiveness in their jobs, destroys potential career opportunities, limits their social lives, and hampers them in other social settings as it stops them from fully expressing their thoughts, feelings, and ideas in front of others.

The fear of public performance afflicts not only individuals who are timid and socially anxious, but also those who are otherwise seen as confident and outgoing. Many people go to great lengths to avoid speaking up in front of groups, either formally or informally. Or if they do speak they are far are less effective than they could be if they had managed the fear with the proper tools.

This fear strongly affects an individual's professional life and prospects for career advancement. This performance anxiety isn't just in the area of public speaking but also musical and theatrical performance where it is probably more prevalent. People working in the performing arts and entertainment fields, such as singers, musicians, and actors, experience performance anxiety.

Even some of the most talented and accomplished performers may suffer from intense performance anxiety and feel tremendous fear when anticipating or giving performances (or they may avoid performances altogether).

A survey of 2,212 professional classical musicians indicated that 24% had a problem with performance anxiety, and 16% of these described their problem as severe. However, for the vast majority of people who experience stage fright they do so without any wider problems.

Mark Twain once said, "There are two types of speakers: those that are nervous and those that are liars."

NOTE

Even experienced performers and speakers have stage fright. A partial list of famous people with performance anxiety includes Abraham Lincoln, Jonathan Knight, Adele, Carly Simon, Barbra Streisand, Amanda Seyfried, Andrea Bocelli, Rod Stewart, Lawrence Olivier, Glenn Gould, Annie Lennox, Paul Newman, and Donny Osmond. While I am not in the famous category, I do have something in common with the people on this list—I have performance anxiety.

Many people have given up professional opportunities for advancement because the new position calls for more public speaking or public performance. Some people have left a job or have not gone on for higher education to avoid facing their fear. There is clearly much lost potential for individuals, and for society, due to this fear.

Having this fear also takes a big toll on the person's self-confidence and self-esteem, as many people feel embarrassed and ashamed to have such a fear. They may try to keep their fear hidden as much as possible, though they are often afraid of being "found out." They are often intensely uncomfortable and self-conscious with being "in the spotlight" and having others focus attention on them.

A deep fear associated with public speaking or performing is the *fear of embarrassment* and *negative evaluation by others*. Many people feel terrified of making a fool of themselves in front of others and fear that people will view them as inadequate in some way. There is often a fear of harsh judgment from others, and a fear of loss of credibility and respect if others find out just how afraid they are. Many people who suffer this fear tend toward perfectionism and are afraid to make mistakes. They are afraid to let others see their fear and vulnerability, fearful of not being seen as strong and in control.

While a person can often successfully avoid situations that require public speaking or performing, the avoidance behavior itself actually worsens the fear. The person comes to believe that she cannot handle speaking or performing situations and that avoidance is the only solution. While the avoidance may initially provide a feeling of great relief, it nevertheless erodes the person's self-confidence and belief in herself and thus greatly limits and constricts the person's life choices.

NOTE

An avoidance of the fear does not make it go away or in any way improve the quality of your life. However, channeling it can give you a way to release great passion. Audiences love this and will love you for it.

The layman's definition of stage fright is the fear of performing in front of others that is the result of high intensity emotion or the extra energy that is trying to flow through your body when you become the center of attention. It absolutely is not an indication that you are a weak person lacking conviction, a coward, or a bad speaker or presenter. Instead it is a sign that you have a lot of creative emotional energy that, as of yet, you just don't know how to use and express to your benefit. This can be managed, and your nervous energy can be channeled into a positive force.

Having stage fright is one thing; doing something about it and using it to your advantage is another. It is nonsense to tell you to just conquer or overcome your stage fright. Instead, there is a better strategy to consider if you feel the pangs of stage fright, and that is to recognize it and use it to your advantage.

Fear is a common human feeling. How we manage and deal with fear is an important step with regard to making the ten steps discussed in this book work for you.

Strategy: Try to Quantify the Fear

> **NOTE**
>
> Mark Twain said: "My life has been filled with calamities, some of which actually happened." There's a study that proves we fear and worry about way more than actually occurs. Researchers at the University of Cincinnati found that *85% of what people worry about never happens.* Moreover, the study found that 79% of us handle the 15% that does happen in ways that surprise us with our ability to turn the situation around so that the outcome almost never is a bad as we imagined (Ekman, 1989).

While we sometimes laugh at ourselves after the fact, the act of worrying is no laughing matter. Worrying causes serious problems, especially performance anxiety. The reactions flood the brain with stress hormones. In its worse form and with long-term exposure, worry can make us prone to disease and some emotional problems. Stress hormones also debilitate higher brain functions, dampening memory, the capacity to learn, and the ability to sustain peak performance.

The part of the primitive brain in charge of stress reactions is our old friend the amygdala. This organ is fully developed in a human being by age two. The intelligence of the primitive brain is at the level of a two-year-old. When a worried person frets and ruminates over the smallest matter, we often say the person is acting like a two-year-old. That description is not far from the truth. Neurologically, this is the system that's in charge.

> **NOTE**
>
> When we're worried or under stress, all we see are problems and not the solutions. But once we've quieted the brain, control shifts from the lower to the higher brain where creative intelligence kicks in. We can start to see solutions and we feel and perform better. A simple tool is the powerful first step in rewiring the brain to extinguish worry at the point of inception.

Let's quantify what is going on with performance anxiety and then we tackle it piece by piece with the most effective strategies and tactics.

Anxiety is the vague uncomfortable feeling mixing dread, fear, and even danger from something we feel we don't have control over. Before man developed his cerebral cortex, our first brain, the amygdala, just provided a bicameral emotional option—the fight or flight response. Our response to anxiety was physical—either run or fight. Excess adrenaline was discharged from the adrenal glands to help facilitate either action. Over millions of years the human brain developed thinking, reasoning, learning, insight, and language, but the amygdala still remains the emotional trigger.

Today when the amygdala senses anxiety it still sends the auto response to fight or run but in partnership with the thinking brain there is a recognition of the need to prioritize the causes of our anxiety and then prepare us to deal with it with the proper proportional response. We can use the anxiety to help improve our performance and allow us to avoid dangerous situations. Symptoms of anxiety may include

- Feeling that something undesirable or harmful is about to happen (edginess and apprehension)

- Blurred vision

- Dry mouth, swallowing difficulty, hoarseness, raspy voice

- Rapid breathing and rapid heartbeat, palpitations

- Twitching or trembling of the hands or legs

- Weakness in the legs

- Muscle tension, headaches, and backache

- Sweating hands and face

- Difficulty concentrating

- Dizziness or fainting

- Nausea, diarrhea, or weight loss

- Sleeplessness or fatigue

- Irritability

Here is a simple way to hopefully alter your thinking about your stage fright and quantify it.

The graphic in Figure 2.1 is an exercise I have used for years with my clients and students to help them understand that the fear of public speaking can be faced more rationally and managed to our benefit. This can happen if we understand that the fear of public speaking, like the vast majority of our fears and worries, will almost always be worse than actually speaking in public.

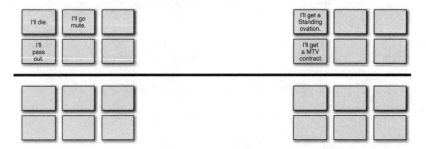

1. On the left of the horizontal line write in any **negative or bad** outcomes that you can imagine might occur as a result of of your stage fright during your next speech or presentation. Note: I have already entered a couple that my students always include.

2. On the right of the horizontal line write in any **positive or good outcome** you can imagine might occur as a result of your stage fright during your next speech or presentation. Note: I have already entered a couple that my students always include.

Figure 2.1 The reality of stage fright

After filling in the left (negative) and right (positive) possibilities, study the diagram and absorb the visual impact of this data. After looking at this for some time your consciousness will begin to absorb the beginnings of the reality that neither extreme (1) nor (2) is likely. Neither the very worst nor the very best of what your imagination is dealing with is likely to occur. Instead, as in the overwhelming vast majority of cases, your experience will be somewhere in the middle.

Will your presentation be perfect without mistakes or errors? That would be the ultimate experience, but it's probably not going to happen. Mistakes are made by even the top speakers and presenters all the time. The key is to keep going. Most of the time the audience won't know when you have made a mistake—unless you volunteer the information and why would you want to do that?

I am not suggesting you can suddenly become fearless, charge the podium, overcome your fear of speaking in public, and deliver flawless, perfect presentations hereafter. However, there is a process that can help you understand what you are dealing with, manage the fear, and rechannel it into a form that the audience sees and experiences as controlled energy and passion.

In my life I have viewed thousands of speeches, and I have never seen or heard of anyone dying, going mute, passing out, going blind, vomiting, being suddenly struck with stammering, or suddenly speaking in tongues as a result of their stage fright. The worse that you imagine simply will not occur.

It will help if you develop a simple strategy to deal with performance anxiety. If you do not suffer at all from performance anxiety, your strategy is even simpler: Move on to the preparation of your speech or presentation with the confidence that you can manage any nervousness that occurs.

If you recognize that you have some level of performance anxiety the strategy needs to be to identify the level and then focus on tactics and approaches to minimize its effects. Studies have shown that up to 25% to 30% of people probably feel some level of anxiety related to the fear of public speaking. It is important to recognize that while the levels of anxiety and the fears are real they range from mild to moderate and are all manageable without medications or therapy.

Strategy: Take Preventative Steps

There are a number of preventive steps you can take if the fear of public speaking begins to show itself.

- Have a favorite poem or phrase (yoga refers to this as a mantra) that you can recite to yourself just before you speak. This can calm your nerves and give you confidence.

- Make sure to avoid dairy products up to 10 to 12 hours before speaking. Dairy products can create mucus in the throat, so absence of dairy products eliminates this obstacle.

- Avoid chocolate and caffeine products for up to 4 hours before your speak. Your body will be producing an abundance of adrenaline, so you don't want to take in any food products that cause your body to produce more.

- Do isometric exercises a few minutes before you are announced. These are exercises you can do from your chair. It involves tightening different major muscle groups for 10 to 12 seconds then relaxing them. Do this for 2 to 4 minutes.

- Open your jaw as wide as possible and hold in this position for 60 seconds. Then close it slowly touching just your outer lips. This relaxes your jaw, which may be tight from nervous tension, and it opens the sinus cavities in the nasal areas.

- Warm up your voice and tongue by reciting tongue twister rhymes and yawning wide. Following are some tongue twisters I have been using for years:

- Little Lilly laid a lump on the lip of Larry for leaving her alone.

- Sad Sally sat still in the subway on Sunday sipping a soda.

- Fuzzy wuzzy was a bear; fuzzy wuzzy had no hair; fuzzy wuzzy wasn't fuzzy was he?

- Tall Tom took a trip to Topeka on Tuesday and traveled there on a train.

- Zipping a zipper before supper is sometimes a zany silly stunt.

- Willy won't want to wait for winter to wrangle the rest of the worms.

- Peter Piper picked a peck of pickled peppers. How many peppers did Peter Piper pick?

Strategy: Get Angry and Punish the Fear

People with performance anxiety could borrow a tactic used by some doctors to help cancer patients come to grips with their disease and use the power of the mind to help fight it. The tactic is simply to draw a picture of the villain (either cancer cells, or in the case of performance anxiety, some icon or cartoon character that represents the anxiety). Then with scissors or marking pens disfigure, mark up, color out, and destroy the symbol of the anxiety.

Strategy: Think of the Audience as Your Home Field Advantage

One of the most important realities and truths you need to take to heart is your audience wants you to succeed. Most of them are happy they are not up there where you are, so they are rooting for you to do well. Recognize there is an energy coming from the audience just like there is at a sporting event with the home team. If you relax a little you will be able to sense the encouragement, the support. It is like the home field advantage many sports teams use as an extra player.

If you can, arrive early at the place where you will be speaking or presenting and go out and meet some of the audience. If you meet and speak with a few people, it is easier to think of them as acquaintances and friendly fans than as strangers. Connecting with the audience lets them see you as friendly and accessible people, not distant experts.

Strategy: Prepare and Write Your Own Introduction

Unless the event planner is experienced and well organized your bio is a subtle but critically important part of the presentation that can be overlooked. You should be asked for your bio well in advance of the event. If you are not, be proactive and provide it to the person who will be handling your introduction.

Take your time and plan your written bio. This biographical information provides your audience with their clue as to who you are, including your background, experience, and interests. These are all things your audience wants to know about you before you speak. This is your chance to begin the branding or the creation of the image projection you want to make on the audience.

Strategy: Practice, Practice, Practice

Part of what makes performance anxiety such a real thing to us is the audience is real. The people in the audience are not an abstraction or made a distant vague entity by the filter of TV, radio, or the computer. They are real because we can see and hear them. They could be friends, acquaintances, professional peers, a class full of students, or even a room full of wedding guests. So stepping out onto a stage is the real thing, and it often can bring the real form of anxiety. One effective strategy is to prepare so well that your confidence in your subject overcomes much of the fear.

Prior to your speech or presentation, practice the speech as you would actually deliver it a minimum of six complete times to ensure you have the timing, pace, rhythm, and information down comfortably. In addition to practicing the presentation, the speech should be practiced over and over again in your mind's eye—your imagination. Try to envision the entire event from your introduction to your presentation to the conclusion in every detail as you would like to see it happen. Play this back over and over again. This is called productive distraction.

An abbreviated version of this strategy is to practice your introduction and the first few minutes of your speech or presentation so you are comfortable with that portion. The point behind this strategy is that for many people affected by performance anxiety the fear seems to dissipate somewhat after a minute or two.

The closer it gets to the time for the presentation, try to surround yourself with people with positive attitudes. Read stories, books, and articles and watch television programs and movies about people who were successful in their endeavors. You want to minimize the anticipation. For many people the anticipatory anxiety can become as debilitating as the actual performance anxiety. Therefore try to stay calm and not get anxious about feeling anxious.

Most of the Signs of Stage Fright Can Be Managed Quickly and Silently

I can't emphasize enough that even though the fear of public speaking is real and only some of the symptoms are visible, your success in managing the fear nevertheless must be planned for and dealt with through real management plans. You must have strategies and tactics that are planned out, practiced, and executed when necessary. Don't let performance anxiety sneak up on you. Even if you believe that since you have never felt it before, you will never fall victim to it in the future, a little preparation will come in handy. Some major movie, sports, entertainment, and stage stars have performed for decades and suddenly out of nowhere were struck with performance anxiety. Knowing some preventive actions can help.

Many of the symptoms of stage fright can be directly related to your breathing, either breathing too quickly (hyperventilation) or breathing too shallowly (hypoventilation, also known as respiratory depression, occurs when ventilation is inadequate). Awareness of your breathing can help reduce some tension caused by your body reacting to too much or too little air.

A few minutes before your speech, find someplace quiet and alone. Close your eyes and rest with your feet flat on the floor. Beginning with the top of your head and then going down to your toes, imagine your body drifting on a cloud or a wave until you have disappeared in total relaxation.

Focus your mind's eye on your image of your speech or presentation coming off as a complete success.

Be aware of your breathing. Breathe in through your nose and out through your mouth slowly. You are looking to find a comfortable breathing pattern which you can maintain throughout your speech or presentation.

As you are being introduced, tighten all the muscle groups in your body for a couple of seconds, then relax them all and go do your speech.

Trembling or Shaking

People's hands can tremble and shake, causing their notes or pages to rustle noisily. This common reaction to stage fright can be managed by laying the notes down on the podium or holding them against your body until you are ready to glance at them again.

Do not put your hands in your pockets or rest them on your hips to prevent or stop your hands from trembling. These gestures are not only poor posture but also send negative body language signals of boredom and/or defensive blocking to your audience.

Avoid touching your face or head with your hands. Most facial and head touching have negative body language connotations. For example, touching the nose is called the Pinocchio Effect and is interpreted as the speaker is lying. Touching or grabbing the ear suggests "I am not listening, or I can't hear or I don't want to hear this." Grasping the hands or fingers into a steepling or praying gesture has an implication of "I am closing or locking you out." Hands or fingers touching, stroking, or covering the mouth says, "I am trying to cover up what I am saying because I don't believe it, or I have no confidence in it, or I am lying."

Obviously an occasional touch of your face or head is not an issue; it is the continual or frequent actions that distract and signal your audience.

Mind Going Blank

People do occasionally forget their place in their speech, but that is where notes come in or having previously memorized key words that act as road signals to help you recall where you are in your speech or presentation. This is why I recommend frequent practice and having a thorough knowledge of the topic. Knowing the topic and having gone over the speech or presentation many times can give you the confidence that you can find the right word or phrase to connect you to the right point.

Completely forgetting one's place in a speech or presentation and being unable to find the place in the notes can be managed by resorting to a *safe word* or phrase the speaker has practiced and knows or has written down. The safe word or phrase leads the speaker to a completely safe topic or point that he or she can mention and spend time on for as long as necessary to either get back on topic or link to a place where it is appropriate to close the speech in a reasonable time.

If you find yourself unable to pick up where you were and are stuck at some point, and there is absolutely no way out, I advise speakers and presenters to (1) pause as if in thought; (2) locate the next speech or presentation point or topic; and (3) simply say, "and now I want to move on to… (my next point, the final point)." No one in the audience will know what just happened—that is, unless you tell them, and why would you want to do that?

Doing or Saying Something Disconcerting

The more practice you put in and the more knowledge you have about a topic, the less likely it is that you might say or do something disconcerting. However, it is possible, and every speaker from the best, most experienced speaker to the beginner will at some time do or say something that has the potential to be disconcerting. This includes, but is not limited to, mispronouncing a common word, transposing a well-known phrase, stuttering, misquoting a famous quote, misstating an obvious point, having your voice crack, or hyperventilating.

The best strategy is to accept that this is your small human mistake. You deal with it by a smile or a light laugh if appropriate and move on. The audience will appreciate you more if you just acknowledge your mistake rather than let such an incident ruin your speech or presentation. A tremor or crack in your voice is usually a physical manifestation generally a result of stage fright. People do occasionally get tremors in their voice, but by dropping your head slightly and taking a breath you can quickly reduce or eliminate these effects.

Speakers and presenters can start to hyperventilate if they become too nervous. This is another symptom of uncontrolled stage fright. If this happens simply pause or slow down, make eye contact with a friendly set of eyes, smile, take a deep breath using your diaphragm not you upper lungs, pause, and then go on. You can also take a drink of water (from a glass) giving you time to relax and take a breath.

Being Unable to Talk Due to Dry Mouth or Coughing

People who are nervous can easily get a dry mouth or throat and even develop a cough. It is permissible to bring a glass (not a bottle) of room temperature water preferably with a slice of lemon to the podium and to take a drink before the speech or presentation. If necessary you can take a drink after making a point or during a pause in your remarks. The pause for a drink can also give you a few seconds to recover and breathe.

Some actors and beauty contestants use a tactic that you could try that keeps their lips from becoming dry and as an added bonus gives them bright sparkling teeth. The tip is to spread just a *tiny* dab of Vaseline gel on their teeth.

Another tip to help avoid a dry mouth is to lightly bite the tip of your tongue. This biting simulation helps the mouth secrete moisture. Be careful not to take a chunk out of your tongue because this will not only be painful but will cause your tongue to swell making speaking even more difficult. It is advisable to practice this a few times before your speech or presentation so you get the hang of it.

One way some people have of dealing with their stress of performance anxiety is by movement—not just by any movement but by excessive movements. The real problem here is any movement in front of an audience, especially from an elevated stage is magnified and exaggerated in the eyes of the audience because they are so focused on you. So let's deal with the exaggerated movement issues first.

Pacing Too Much

People who are dealing with their nervousness can sometimes begin to pace back and forth in front of an audience. Another form of pacing is rocking forward and backward or side-to-side. Not only is this excessive body movement a distraction to the audience, it can increase the speaker's or presenter's nervousness and even increase the chances of losing one's balance. Some movement in front of an audience isn't bad and in fact can be effective if you are doing so when you are trying to make a particularly important point that you want the audience to remember. Movement while speaking should be based on your decision and with you in control.

To help you overcome the tendency to pace, here are a couple of suggestions. If you can arrive early and are able to survey the speaking area and it is appropriate, you can lay down pieces of tape that you can easily spot if you begin to wander too far; see the diagram in Figure 2.2.

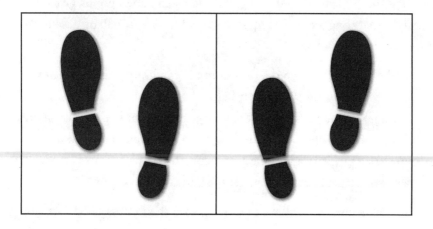

Figure 2.2 The ready stance and boundaries to avoid wandering too far from your speaking space

The tape can be a reminder to anchor yourself, or you can add an icon on the tape that reminds you to stop pacing. Another approach is you can make a comment in the margin of your notes to remind yourself "Don't pace."

Rocking Back and Forth on One's Heels and Toes

If you know from experience or someone telling you that you have a tendency to rock back and forth on your toes and heels, you can use the same approach as suggested for too much pacing. Just place the tape in front of where you would normally stand.

Or, make yourself a notation in the margin of your notes.

An old standby is to have a friend or coach in the audience clearly visible to the speaker who can subtly send sign language signals that you are rocking or swaying, or bending repeatedly.

Swaying from Side to Side or Bending Low at the Waist Repeatedly

These issues are similar to the situations already discussed, and the solution can be the same—place tape on the floor to remind you not to sway or add a note in the margins of your speech. Another self-correcting solution for this mannerism is to tape three or four 1-inch wooden dowels to each side of your waist, and when you bend or sway you will feel the dowels and be reminded you've moved too far.

Not Smiling or Flashing or Holding a Half Smile (the Thin Smile)

We mention the importance of smiling many times and still it can't be emphasized enough. It is probably the single most critical nonverbal signal a speaker can use to communicate. Conversely, not smiling is probably the single worst nonverbal signal a speaker can communicate. Not smiling is at best a signal of being cold and distant or bored, defiant, or angry.

Not smiling is bad, but certain kinds of smiling can be even worse. The half-smile or the thin smile is seen as deceptive, sinister, and devious. The famous *Mona Lisa* sports the coy half smile. What is she hiding? It might make for an interesting portrait, but you don't want your audience wondering that when you speak. Another problematic smile is the so-called grin, with the lower teeth showing, eyes wide like a deer in the headlights, and no crow's feet or wrinkles near the eyes showing control over the expression.

The fake smile, also known as the model's flash or the frozen smile, is another smile you want to avoid in your speech. This is the classic fake smile used by runway models or people with something to hide. The bottom teeth are displayed and no muscles are in use around the eyes or upper lips.

Two facial muscle groups are important to us in determining a real smile from a fake smile. The Zygomatic major muscles control the lifting of the face at the mouth and show the upper teeth. Other muscle groups are not activated in a true smile but are activated in a fake smile, and these muscles show the lower teeth.

The second facial muscle group that helps the real smile are those that control the muscles on the outside portion of the eyes. The saying her "eyes light up or sparkle" when she smiles is a reflection of these muscles acting on the eyes.

Extreme Arm and Hand Gestures

One of the most common visual indicators of a speaker or presenter with stage fright is one who stands rigidly erect at the podium, also called the totem, with his notes held down on the podium shelf. The opposite is one who slouches as if he is ready to drop off into a deep sleep. Occasionally performance anxiety might display itself as extremely wild arm or hand gestures. Some of the common gestures of speakers experiencing stage fright are discussed in this section.

Gestures that include touching the head and face repeatedly generally send negative body language cues. Touching the forehead is body language that says I am dumbfounded. Touching the nose is the Pinocchio gesture and signals a speaker who is not telling the truth. Grabbing or touching the ears sends the signal I don't hear or can't hear the truth. Touching or covering the mouth sends the signal that the speaker is hiding her words that are not true. Hands or palms to the side of the face signals despair.

Hands and palms extended outward to the audience is the stop sign or the push back sign symbolizing that the speaker desires to be finished with the audience and wants to turn them out. Any hand or arm gesture above the head is visually awkward and sends aggressive signals. The finger point is a negative scolding accusatory signal, and the double finger point doubles this signal.

There is nothing wrong with using hand and arm gestures if they are done properly to emphasize certain points that the speaker is making and they follow simple guidelines of nonverbal communications.

If you want to emphasize an important point it is recommended and perfectly acceptable to make a motion with one of the speaker's fists in a downward motion either from a position no higher than the chest to a point no lower than the waist or into the open palm of the other hand. A speaker can use one motion or two, but more than that and the fist gesture emphasis begins to take on the appearance of anger or rage, and unless that is the emotion you want the audience to feel, don't do it.

Speakers should avoid all hand and arm gestures above the head or below the waist. Those gestures are unusual, and there is no way to keep them from looking awkward. Besides, these types of gestures generally have a negative connotation attached so they should be avoided.

Speakers should try to avoid any movement of the hands and arms that emanate from the shoulders. If a gesture is going to be made, make it from the elbow.

As previously mentioned, speakers should try to avoid gestures that involve face touching. With the exceptions of stroking the chin (which has the nonverbal language meaning "I'm thinking or considering what is being said") and the single finger tapping the temple (same meaning), most all other face and head touching nonverbal language is a negative sign.

As a rule of thumb, the more nervous the speaker is, fewer gestures are better.

Using Word or Phrase Fillers

One of the most common traits that even slips into the most experienced speaker's bad habit category is repeated use of filler words or phrases. Examples of the most common filler words, phrases, and sounds are

- "Hum"
- "Ah"
- "OK"
- "All right"
- "Wow"
- "Gee"
- "Listen up"
- "Yes"
- "Absolutely"
- "Tremendous"
- "Grand"
- "Like"
- "You know"
- "Er"
- "Right"
- "Look here"
- "Zap"
- "Whew"
- Clicking of the teeth
- Sucking noises
- Excessive clearing of the throat

There are other fillers and sounds, and some speakers even develop their own personal made up words. These are really fillers or ways speakers fill oral space when they fear a pause or silence between thoughts, phrases, or sentences. For some reason, some speakers feel the need to fill the room with sound every moment. There are legitimate and effective uses of silence, but for some speakers silence is uncomfortable, and usually an unconscious tick results and a filler word sneaks in.

For the audience it isn't noticeable unless they are looking for it or it becomes chronic—more than two or three times a minute. President Obama is guilty of this. He does it even with teleprompter scripted remarks and is even worse with off-the-cuff comments. Once, in a 2-minute comment, I heard him utter the filler words "ah" or "um" 23 times.

When filler words become chronic, they become a deadly distraction to the audience, which starts to pay more attention to the filler words and to their frequency than to what the speaker is actually trying to say.

The correction to filler words creeping in to a speaker's presentation is awareness. This requires a friend or coach to observe and monitor the speaker and first count the filler words letting the speaker know how often they are occurring. Next the friend or coach can record the speaker and let the speaker hear the filler words.

Usually just a few sessions of someone reminding the speaker of the bad habit greatly reduces the use of the filler words. Also, continued practice of the speech and presentation along with choreographed points of planned pauses and silence helps.

Not Filling the Audience Chamber with the Proper Speaking Volume

Every audience chamber is slightly different in size, acoustics, number of people in attendance, and where they are sitting relative to the speaking space. Regardless of whether the speaker is using a microphone, it is the speaker's responsibility to fill the audience chamber with the appropriate speaking volume.

The appropriate speaking volume is a level at which the speaker speaking in his normal volume can be easily heard by the audience members in the farthest row. In a relatively large chamber, speakers who have normally low or breathy voices will have to adjust their speaking volumes up. On the other hand, speakers with deep, booming voices may have to tone down their volume to a more moderate volume and slightly higher pitch than their norm in that situation.

Sweating of the Face and Hands

Nervousness can cause some people to sweat and show the perspiration on their face and cause their hands to become damp. It is a good idea to carry a handkerchief so that perspiration can be blotted from your face and hand. Handkerchiefs should be used folded and not open. They should be as inconspicuous as possible and used during a pause in your comments. Speakers can also apply talcum power to their hands just prior to speaking to keep hands dry.

Excessive Sweating of Underarms

If a speaker's nervousness causes excessive body perspiration the inside lining of a suit or dress may become so damp it could become visible to the audience. Extra deodorant just before speaking time can help in these situations.

Shaky or Weak Legs

Performance anxiety can manifest itself in the feeling the speaker or presenter is figuratively on shaky ground; her legs may feel shaky or even weak and may be unable to sustain the speaker. This is psychological and can be managed by movement such as walking away from the podium. The speaker or presenter can use the movement to overcome the shaky leg feeling and make a point, doing two things at once.

Grumbling Stomach

Nervousness can manifest itself in rumbling in the stomach. I recommend *not* eating just prior to speaking. (Remember the finite amount of blood in the body is going to where the body needs it, and we want as much blood flowing to the brain as possible, not to the digestive system where digestion can cause drowsiness.) An empty nervous stomach can begin to make some noise. Extra water and/or an over-the-counter antacid lozenge can be taken.

Urge to Tell Jokes or Funny Stories

Inexperienced speakers sometimes attempt to open their remarks with a joke or a humorous story. My advice is don't try this. Not that there isn't a place for humor in public speaking—there is—but only if speaker is experienced and has a well-developed sense of timing and good self-image.

Humor is a doubled-edged sword; it's fine if you're knowledgeable, experienced, have a great sense of timing, know the audience, and know how to tell a joke or funny story especially on yourself. But humor used inappropriately or with the wrong timing can be deadly for an inexperienced speaker. If the joke or humor causes you to lose the audience, an inexperienced speaker will never win them back. Humor therefore carries too much risk, so don't add to the existing anxiety. Leave humor for another place and time.

Key Takeaways

- The fear of public speaking is real. Although performance anxiety is natural and is present in almost everyone, it can be managed and used to help you.

- The audience is your friend; they want you to succeed, so tune into their energy.

- Prior to your speech or presentation, practice the speech as you would actually deliver it a minimum of six complete times to ensure you have the timing, pace, and information down comfortably.

- In addition to actually practicing the speech or presentation, you should also practice over and over again in your mind's eye—your imagination. See your success over and over again.

- Surround yourself with positive people and feelings prior to your speech or presentation.

- Most of the signs of stage fright can be successfully managed quickly and silently.

- Just prior to your speech or presentation, avoid carbonated soda, coffee, and caffeine.

- Just prior to your presentation try not to eat. You want maximum blood flow to your brain, not to your digestive system.

- A few minutes before your speech find someplace quiet and alone. Close your eyes and rest with your feet flat on the floor. Beginning with the top of your head and then going down to your toes, imagine your body drifting on a cloud or a wave until you have disappeared in total relaxation.

- Focus your mind's eye on your image of total success—your speech or presentation coming off as a complete success.

- Be aware of your breathing, breathe in through your nose and out through your mouth slowly.

- As you are being introduced, tighten all the muscle groups in your body for a couple of seconds, then relax them all and go do your speech.

Chapter 2 Notes

Currie, Keith Allan. 2001. Performance Anxiety Coping Skills Seminar: Is It Effective in Reducing Musical Performance Anxiety and Enhancing Musical Performance Quality? Dissertation, Virginia Tech.

Ekman, Paul. 1989. The Argument and Evidence about Universals in Facial Expression of Emotion. In *Handbook of Social Psychophysiology*, ed. H. Wagner and A. Manstead, 143-164. Chichester: John Wiley & Sons.

Kelly, Kevin. 2010. *What Technology Wants*. New York: Viking Press.

Leahy, Robert, Ph.D., 2000. *The Worry Cure*. New York: Random House.

3

Step 3: Prepare Immediately and Prepare for a Conversation, Not a Speech

It usually takes me more than three weeks to prepare a good impromptu speech.

—Mark Twain (Source: Facebook.com/authorstream)

The moment has arrived. You have been selected, picked, assigned, required, or otherwise found yourself in a position where you will be asked or required to stand up before a group of people and speak. This occurs more frequently for students than others, but almost everyone will face the situation in which you have to make a presentation or speech. Communication skills are seen by executives and hiring managers as the most sought after skill in new hires and as such are considered one of the most important career development skills.

Whether you recognize it or not, the chance to speak in front of an audience is an opportunity. You have been given an opportunity to set and achieve a difficult goal. I have observed that most people who complete their speaking experience feel great accomplishment and satisfaction afterward. Goal achievement is a major step in improving one's mental health.

When you know you have to speak mark your calendar and begin preparing immediately. The following calendar chart is a suggested aid to help you track your timeline to success. The matrix is simple to read and use. Table 3.1 is an example of the chart.

Table 3.1   Countdown to Your Speech or Presentation

Today's Date	Total Days to Event	Planning Objective	Compete by Date	Completed Y, N (If no, why?)
April 1	100	Get notebook to record creative ideas on speech topic.	April 1	Y
April 7	94	Transfer initial creative ideas from notebook to laptop.	April 7	Y

Do not succumb to the temptation to put off preparation because it is an unpleasant task. Start immediately by thinking and then making notes (get yourself a small notebook or journal) to jot down ideas that come to mind. Or if you feel more comfortable with your iPad or mobile device use it. The important thing is to get ideas and thoughts down. Don't worry about structure or sentences or order or context. All that will come later; for now it's just ideas.

Unless you have been given a topic on which to speak, you can help control some of the anxiety of public speaking by choosing your own topic or something with which you already have some familiarity. Even if you are given a topic it generally will be a broad overarching topic and you have or should ask for the leeway to influence the final content. You should select a topic you are familiar with and passionate about.

I often hear my students and clients complain that they don't really know that much about anything well enough to speak publically on the topic. (This is really their fear talking.) I have the solution for them. The following exercise shows how just about any word or phrase can lead to multiple topic choices.

When people see the multiple topics that can result from a single word, they are encouraged to try the same exercise with a couple of words themselves and invariably, a topic comes to them.

Finding Multiple Topics from a Single Word

The root word is the starting point (see Figure 3.1). From the root word begin to think and write down all concepts, ideas, words, themes—anything related to the root word in any way. Then from these do the same thing until you have exhausted all possibilities. You will be surprised at how far afield any word can take you (see Figure 3.2).

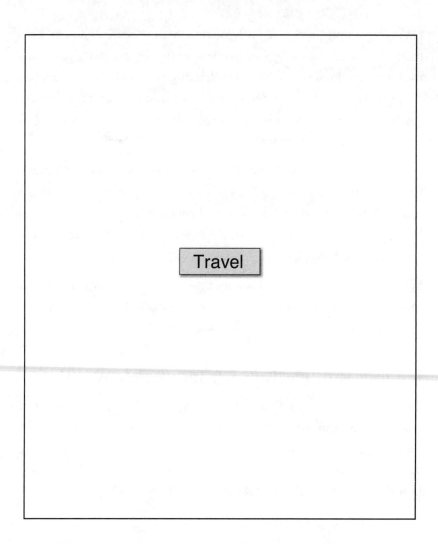

Figure 3.1 A single word can be the source of multiple topics

As this figure shows the single word "travel" expanded in a rational thought process can take you to multiple themes and topics including "Performance Anxiety."

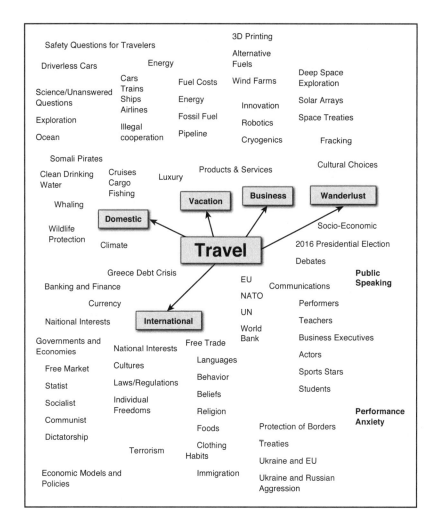

Figure 3.2 Multiple themes and topics from the single word "travel"

When we have a goal to accomplish, our unconscious mind begins to stir and send images, thoughts, ideas, concepts, and even half-baked ideas to our conscious mind. For most of us these ideas come when we least expect them. They come during the quiet moments: when we are in the shower, dreaming, eating, sitting quietly, walking, exercising, praying, just waking up, and other times.

Our unconscious mind is trying to help us by sorting, retrieving, filtering, and sending us what it believes is helpful data. If we don't write this data (ideas and flashes) down in all probability we will lose it (forget it) and probably will never recall it again. It is likely in a day or two we will remember we had a great idea or an interesting thought that would be good to use, but we will never remember the actual idea or thought. It can be terribly frustrating, but we can avoid this frustration by writing down our thoughts.

If you are open to receiving it, your unconscious mind sends you raw unfiltered data. This data may need additional thought and even some research and background checking to turn it into information that is useful for your purpose—content for your speech or presentation.

Of course, depending on the subject matter, topic, audience profile, or actual assignment you will probably have to conduct further research, fact checking, or other background checking work to ensure you have all that you need for your speech or presentation content.

Don't go crazy with your content preparation. You will be surprised at how much you already know about most of the topics on which you will be asked to speak. You also will know the length of your speech or presentation. With this knowledge and the fact that audiences simply are not capable of remembering more than three or four major points you have some idea of what can be covered—not a lot and certainly not a lot of detailed facts and figures.

Unless the audience is prepared to attend a specific rhetorical event, such as an annual speech, political event, graduation or honors ceremony, or acceptance speech for an honor, you will make them a happy group if you make your presentation a conversation with them. In such a conversation, the more stories you tell, the more case studies you relate to the main points you want to get across, and the more examples you can give, the more organized your speech will be and the better it will be received and remembered. Who wouldn't want to be better prepared, have an easier job presenting, and be more effective?

If you prepare as though you were going to just stand up and talk with family or friends for up to 50 minutes, your actual speech or presentation is more likely to be delivered as a conversation, using a conversational tone. You will be more comfortable and relaxed and so will your audience. Who will be in the audience? People who fear public speaking themselves and are glad they are not where you are. A speech or presentation delivered in a conversational manner puts them at ease and makes them more receptive to your comments.

Remember, your audience wants you to succeed. They are your friend and your home team advantage.

The Audience and How to Converse with Them

What is the make-up of the audience? Who will be in the audience? What is the profile or what are the interests, concerns, and agenda of the people who will be listening to your speech or presentation?

This information will help guide what you want to say and how you want to say it. There are a variety of different styles of speeches and presentations, such as informative, invitational, persuasive, inspirational, motivational, small group, testimonial, provocative, award presentation, improvisational, educational, and the list goes on and on.

LEARN TO TELL A STORY

My goal in this book is not to give you the whole body of knowledge regarding public speaking and try to guide you toward the full range of skills, techniques, and abilities of a well-trained experienced speaker. But instead my goal is to help you with just the essential things you can learn quickly. If you put these guidelines into practice they will help get you through your next speech or presentation successfully, and you still can expect to do better than most speakers.

With this in mind, the reality of your situation and your next speaking or presentation opportunity is you are not likely to be faced with the decision of what type of speech or presentation style you'll need.

Your circumstances are more likely to be something like an assignment for which you want to do well, an invitation for career purposes you can't turn down, or something you feel obligated to do for someone.

These situations are entirely different from "speaking engagements" in which fully trained, experienced, or professional speakers work. This is why I have suggested the conversational approach, where you probably are not going to have to worry much about the stylistic aspects or the traditional speaking styles.

Therefore concentrate on developing your next public speaking "conversation" with the accompanying stories, cases, examples, and three to four points you want the audience to remember. This is your goal.

Your audience is even more likely to be friendly because they are most likely going to be made up largely of individuals whom you know or who know you—your home crowd advantage.

Nevertheless, you still want to have some information about who they are, so if possible you will want to customize some of your remarks for them. Nothing warms an audience more than comments or remarks that show you know something about them or you are "one of them." Everyone knows the famous President John F. Kennedy line that lifted the spirits and morale of millions of Germans in June 1963 during the Cold War. Standing before the Berlin Wall he said, "Ich bin ein Berliner," which translated means "I am a citizen of Berlin." Though this is an extreme example, you can see the value of connecting with your audience by knowing to whom you are speaking.

Laying Out What You Are Going to Say and How You Are Going to Say It

Since you have been preparing from the moment you got the notice you were going to be speaking or presenting, you have been making notes of ideas that have come from your unconscious, your own observations, and research. At the point of information saturation (when ideas begin to repeat themselves) you should stop focusing on information gathering and begin to draft or sketch out what you are going to say in your conversation to your audience.

The point of information saturation arrives when your unconscious and or your research begin to turn up the same or similar points repeatedly. At this point it does not make sense to continue your primary focus on idea generation but to switch to getting your thoughts down in some kind of order and the way you want to get them across to the audience.

While I already said I do not want to confuse you with issues of speaking or presentation style now, there is a hint regarding written and spoken communication in general that I have always found helpful, and I will share it with you so perhaps you may find it useful.

NOTE

Rudyard Kipling is the author of this ode that media people have lived by for years. "I had six good men who taught me all I knew. Their names were 'What,' 'When,' 'Where,' 'Why,' 'How,' and 'Who.'" Answering these six questions is an excellent guide for effective communications. Any speech, presentation, conversation, or print content that manages these six questions effectively is usually a success to its audience.

In formal education and training speech classes, textbooks, coaching, and supporting media cover literally dozens of speaking approaches, styles, methods, types, and techniques on giving a speech or making a presentation. Each of these has lists of rules, keys, do's, and don'ts. For a curriculum, workshop, or seminar on public speaking, this methodology is appropriate because students either are required to receive this type of training and education or have requested it.

As previously stated, the vast majority of people don't voluntarily set themselves up for this. However, if a person has to make a speech or a presentation and wants to do the best job possible, there is a way: Keep the speech or presentation simple.

You can get through your next speech or presentation using a simple formula for the organization of your talk. Every speech or presentation should have three distinct parts:

1. **An introduction**—Tell them what you are going to tell them.

2. **The main body**—Tell them.

3. **A conclusion**—Tell them what you told them.

In these three parts, if the speaker or presenter answers the six questions, What, When, Where, Why, How, and Who, the presentation should be a success, and you don't have be concerned about memorizing any of the traditional formal styles, methods, or techniques of public speaking. Just keep it a simple conversation.

There are various opinions as to how much of the total presentation should be devoted to each part, but generally accepted guidelines are 10% of the total time for the introduction, 85% of the total time for the main body, and 5% for the conclusion.

The Introduction

It is important that you are able to clearly separate the three sections for the audience by your words. It is perfectly acceptable to open your speech or presentation with appropriate thanks and other acknowledgments. These kinds of remarks help you settle in and find your voice, pace, tone, and pitch, which linguists call speaking rate, and establish eye contact.

Your introduction sets the overall tone of your comments and unveils the points you will make later. Textbooks offer a variety of options for introductions, including comments on something local, a joke, a quote, a statistic, a Socratic question to the audience, a contemporary or local item of interest, or some other type of opening line. What you decide should be based on one fundament rule and that is *it has to be natural to you.*

NOTE

Don't ever do or try anything someone suggests or recommends as a surefire way to win an audience unless it is something you would do naturally on your own. This advice holds for every aspect of speaking. You have to be yourself. Don't ever attempt to imitate or replicate another person's style—no matter who they are. You must be natural and deliver your speech or presentation in your own style whatever that is.

Be Cautious of Humor

Invariably speakers get advice to use humor to loosen up the audience. My reaction is this isn't a warmup for a TV game show or a comedian. Although humor is a common opening technique, it is something better left to more experienced speakers and presenters who know their audience and know their own skills very well. Humor can work and get a few laughs, but it can also backfire if it is inappropriate, misunderstood, or poorly delivered. It carries too much risk, and the potential for added anxiety for the inexperienced speaker, so I advise leaving it out for now.

For the introduction, figure out what works for you and stick with it. Keep in mind the profile of your audience and what three or four points you plan to make in the body of your speech or presentation. It is completely acceptable to inform your audience in a couple of sentences what you plan to talk to them about. This gives them advance notice of what is to come, and their minds begin to prepare for the information that will be coming.

It cannot be stressed enough that your speech or presentation must be kept as simple as possible. You should think of it as a conversation with a few friends. Keep in mind you have been preparing and researching the topic so you know quite a bit about it. You probably know more than anyone in the audience.

Because you have been reading and studying the topic, terms will become second nature to you, so you want to avoid using industry jargon, technical terms, buzzwords, and any terminology that makes you sound like an industry insider. This advice probably sounds far-fetched because you may be stressed by the idea of speaking. But think about it, how many people have been reading and studying the topic like you? Very few, if any. Remember this. I know you can't imagine an audience feeling intellectually stymied by you, but it can and does happen. You don't want it to happen to you.

You want the audience to feel comfortable and not have to struggle intellectually with trying to figure out what you are talking about. The instant the audience senses you are talking over their heads or above them they will tune you out. They will sit there politely feigning interest, but their interest and attention will have already left the room. In your preparation, simplify, simplify, simplify and then go back and simplify some more.

The introduction covers some opening remarks, including something about you and your background, which is "the who," a brief summary of "the what" you plan to talk about, and some kind of transition comment or statement that leads you into the main body. A transition statement or comment can be a quote, some contemporary reference, another Socratic question, a stated problem, or a statement written just to transition your talk into the main body. It is up to you. Try to use a transition statement that connects the introduction to the main body with words, ideas, themes, and concepts that are obvious. This is not the time to be subtle or creatively obtuse.

Keep in mind that you want to connect emotionally with your audience. Connecting emotionally with listeners isn't something that requires that much thought. It's a natural human inclination; human brains are hard-wired for what experts call *interactional synchrony*. People in a one-to-one conversation quickly fall into a synchrony or balance matching each other's speech rate. As part of an audience, people listening also want to smoothly connect with the speaker's speech patterns and in doing this there is an emotional bond. This bond is strengthened by the speaker's body language—the poise, stature, volume, pitch, rate, tone, and control of the synchrony.

There is an even deeper dimension to this synchrony. In addition to the balance or harmony of the conversation there is something researchers call *motor mimicry*. The power of this is explained by what happens in a room when one person yawns and in a moment others in the room also are yawning. Another example is head nodding. A speaker can get members of the audience nodding approval by the speaker beginning to nod as she speaks. The same principle works with the negative head shake. For the inexperienced speaker, my recommendation is keep it simple and only try this technique with smiling and positive head nods. Obviously it has to be used at appropriate times.

You want the people who are going to be listening to you to get something from the experience. The introduction is the time to tell them why what you are going to say is important or what's in it for them. Having successfully completed the introduction, you are ready to move seamlessly into the main body.

Main Body

My students and clients always ask, "how do I seamlessly move from the introduction to the main body?" The answer is, pause, take a breath, smile, use a transition statement, and just begin the main body. It's that simple.

How you have laid out your ideas and points determines what you say, when you say it, and how you say it. There are dozens of textbook approaches to main body topics, and it is not my goal to try to teach these approaches because they are based on the premise the speaker has chosen a particular speaking or presentation style.

The only advice I have given you is to prepare for a conversation and answer the six questions, What, When, Where, Why, How, and Who. For example, suggest "a what"—issue, problem, or question. A "when" statement or question can follow as well as a "where" statement or question. "Why" and "how" or "who" are ways to introduce possible solutions or answers.

For your conversational approach, I would simply advise mentioning what you want the audience to learn or hear regarding point #1 or issue #1 and then paint a picture with your words. Tell your audience a story, provide a case history, or give them an example that gets your point across. Remember to do the following:

- Be succinct.
- Be colorful.
- Be direct.
- Be passionate.
- Be accurate.
- Be truthful.
- Be brief.

Then be done and move to point #2 and point # 3 and repeat the same approach.

The same formula can be used until you have completed each point you want to cover. At this point you are ready to move to the conclusion.

How Can I Be These Things?

I have repeatedly suggested you try to be simple, but then I just suggested to be colorful and passionate and interesting. Left unsaid are exciting, imaginative, lively, and fascinating. Am I asking you to be dichotomous or different people? The answer is no. You can project all these characteristics, emotions, and more by your rhetoric. One of the five traditional parts (or *canons*) of classical Greek rhetoric concerns control of voice and gestures when giving a speech, meaning both your word choice and your delivery.

By rhetorical style I am referring to the way in which you put your words together, and by delivery I am specifically referring to your pace, tonality, cadence, and pitch. While there are hundreds of rhetorical styles, I purposely am limiting suggestions to just six techniques that can greatly enhance any speech or presentation.

Anaphora

Anaphora is a rhetorical term for the repetition of a word or phrase at the beginning of successive clauses. By building toward a climax, anaphora can create a strong emotional effect. The following are examples of this rhetorical technique:

- "*Of all* the gin joints *in all* the towns *in all* the world, she walks into mine." (Rick Blaine in *Casablanca*)

- "*We shall* go on to the end, *we shall fight* in France, *we shall fight* on the seas and oceans, *we shall fight* with growing confidence and growing strength in the air, *we shall* defend our Island, whatever the cost may be, *we shall fight* on the beaches, *we shall fight* on the landing grounds, *we shall fight* in the fields and in the streets, *we shall fight* in the hills; *we shall* never surrender." (Winston Churchill, speech to the House of Commons, June 4, 1940)

- "*It was the* best of times, *it was the* worst of times, *it was the* age of wisdom, *it was the* age of foolishness, *it was the* epoch of belief, *it was the* epoch of incredulity, *it was the* season of light, *it was the* season of darkness, *it was the* spring of hope, *it was the* winter of despair." (Charles Dickens, *A Tale of Two Cities*)

In addition to giving prominence to ideas in your main thought, the use of the anaphoric technique provides a sense of rhythm and cadence to your presentation. Furthermore it's an aid to memory of key words and terms, so this rhetorical style provides multiple benefits to a speaker.

Alliteration

Alliteration is derived from the Latin, "putting letters together." It is a rhetorical technique in which a number of words, having the same first consonant sound, occur close together in a series.

While this is more commonly found in literary form, it is still an effective oral technique. The following are examples:

- "I watched the bare brown back of the prisoner marching in front of me." (George Orwell, "A Hanging," 1931)

- "The sibilant sermons of the snake as she discoursed upon the disposition of my sinner's soul seemed ceaseless." (Gregory Kirschling, *The Gargoyle*, 2008)

- "Lay, lady, lay, lay across my big brass bed." (Bob Dylan, "Lay, Lady, Lay")

Simile

A *simile* is a figure of speech or an analogy that makes a comparison between two different things that are alike in one way. To help you identify a simile, the words "like" or "as" are always used.

Similes can make our language more descriptive and enjoyable. As a speaker you use similes to add depth and emphasize what you are trying to convey to the listener. Similes can be funny, serious, mean, or creative. Some examples of similes follow:

- Cute as a kitten

- As busy as a bee

- As snug as a bug in a rug

- As happy as a clam

- Life is like a box of chocolates; you never know what you're going to get

- As agile as a monkey

- As black as coal

- As blind as a bat

- My love is like a red, red rose.

- You were as brave as a lion.

- They fought like cats and dogs.

- He is as funny as a barrel of monkeys.

- This house is as clean as a whistle.

- He is as strong as an ox.

Metaphor

Metaphors are a kind of analogy where two unlike things are compared but have something in common. The statement doesn't make sense until you think about it and see the comparison that is being made. Examples of metaphors are

- He's a diamond in the rough. This means he is better than he appears and maybe needs more experience or training to show his true nature.

- She is such an airhead. Airhead implies she is not smart or doesn't think well.

- Time is a thief. There is not enough time to do what you want.

- The world is my oyster. This can mean the speaker is positive about his experiences and is going to do well in life.

- You are a couch potato. This refers to someone who sits and does nothing.

Simile and metaphor can sometimes be confused, so the following examples are included to help you keep them straight:

Simile	Metaphor
Your eyes are like stars.	You are my star.
He eats like a hog.	He is a hog.
You are like a hammer.	You are a hammer.
You are as happy as a baby.	You are a baby.
He is as stubborn as a mule.	He is a mule.
The world is like the theater.	The world is a theater.
Her heart is like ice.	Her heart is ice.
He is as low as snake.	He is a snake.
She disappears like the wind.	She is the wind.
He brays like a sheep.	He is a sheep.
He is as cunning as a wolf.	He is a wolf.

Repetition

Repetition is a rhetorical technique in which the speaker repeats the same words, phrases, or sentences a few times to make an idea clearer, to amplify an idea, or to provide more emphasis on a theme.

Using repetition can make a speech stylistically appealing, but it can also help convey the message in a much more engaging and notable way. It has the ability of making simple sentences with simple language sound more dramatic. It enhances the beauty of a sentence and stresses the point of the main topic with greater significance. Repetition often uses word associations to express ideas and emotions in an indirect manner. Here are examples of the use of repetition:

- Martin Luther King Junior's speech "I Have a Dream" is a famous example, as he repeats "I have a dream" at the beginning of several lines.

- President Roosevelt's December 8, 1941, speech following the Japanese attack on Pearl Harbor, uses repetition in the following passage:

  Yesterday, the Japanese government also launched an attack against Malaya. Last night, Japanese forces attacked Hong Kong. Last night, Japanese forces attacked Guam. Last night, Japanese forces attacked the Philippine Islands. Last night, the Japanese attacked Wake Island. This morning, the Japanese attacked Midway Island (http://www.let.rug.nl/usa/presidents/franklin-delano-roosevelt/pearl-harbor-speech-december-8-1941.php, accessed February 19, 2015).

Analogy

An *analogy* is a comparison of two things, ideas, similes, or metaphors in which each is compared to another thing that is different from the original. An analogy tries to explain an idea or thing by comparing it to something that is familiar. Metaphors and similes are tools used to draw the analogy. Therefore, an analogy is more extensive and elaborate than either a simile or a metaphor. The following are examples of analogy:

- Just as a painter depicts the soul of the person in the portrait, the therapist must show the addict the self-destructive nature of his disease.

- Just as the bat and glove are the tools of the player, the computer and printer are the tools of the sports writer.

- How a ballet dancer interprets a chorographer's work is how a movie producer films a bestselling book.

In addition to the rhetorical techniques discussed speakers have another tool to improve the audience's reception and appreciation of the speech or presentation and that tool is the speaker's delivery or what some people refer to as *cadence*, (that is, pace, tonality, and pitch).

NOTE

There is a message in every speaker's voice. While your words may communicate an idea or a concept, it is your voice (and nonverbal cues) that communicate the meaning and emphasis behind the idea or the message.

From the sound of your voice and the cadence of your words the audience makes judgments about your credibility, interests, beliefs, conviction, and passion about the topics you are presenting and even your attitude toward them. The audience judges your sincerity and credibility in part by your voice, which affects, in a large measure, how they respond to your message.

If your pace, pitch, volume, rhythm, and tonality or timbre of your voice never fluctuate, you are speaking in a monotone. The audience will quickly lose interest in you because a monotone suggests that you have done little preparation for them or in your message. It suggests you don't really care much whether or how your listeners respond.

A change in volume or tone can break a monotone cycle. Also, a change in volume is an effective way to begin a new topic or emphasize an important point.

Pitch is the frequency of the sound waves you produce and how low or high a speaker's voice is used. Speakers should know (by practice) their comfortable pitch range and learn how to move from low to high in their range. Questions, for example, should end on a higher pitch.

Conversely, affirmative statements should end in a level or slightly lower pitch. The ending of statements on a high pitch can create doubt in your listeners. A speaker should vary his pitch throughout a presentation to establish and reinforce the message.

Tempo is the pace at which the speaker delivers her remarks. The speaker should vary the tempo to provide different levels of emphasis throughout the speech or presentation.

A *pause* is an extremely effective communications tool. Most people feel somewhat uncomfortable when a conversation pauses. The same sense of anticipation and expectancy can be effectively used by a speaker.

Pausing just before making a key point creates a dramatic moment the speaker can use to his advantage. Imagine a scenario in which a speaker has been sharing ideas and making effective use of rhyme, tempo, volume, and pitch. Then the speaker looks out into the audience and pauses for 2 to 3 seconds. Then dramatically with volume and gestures makes a vital point.

Audiences Like to Hear about the Speaker

Regardless of the rhetorical technique(s) or words selected, most audiences like connecting the speaker to the main theme or topic. Except for toasts (when the topic is not about the speaker but about the honoree), audiences enjoy connecting with the speaker. This can be facilitated by the speaker offering case studies, examples, and stories of her own life experiences that help make the point or reflect the theme of the presentation.

The Conclusion

Moving to the conclusion is as simple as saying something like, "In conclusion" or "in closing" or "I would like to close with."

The conclusion is a brief opportunity to quickly summarize your important points (that you just told them) and finish with anything you want them to do or "the what." We call these "action steps" or the "call to action." Do you want them to write someone, call someone, go do something, or just think about something? Whatever you want them to do you have to tell them what it is and how to do it. Don't assume they will just know what you want them to do; they won't—you must tell them.

NOTE

In your conclusion if you realize that you missed or failed to make a point during the body of your speech or presentation, *do not* bring it up in the conclusion. Adding something new in the conclusion will only confuse the audience and could cause them to forget one or more of the other important points you just made. If you forgot something in the main body, leave it out.

The conclusion is a good opportunity to use the rhetorical techniques. They are effective devices for use in closing remarks.

Speaking Time

The amount of time you should spend on each point depends on the amount of time you have been given for your speech or presentation. You should know the total time you have when you are given the speaking assignment. Make sure this information is accurate. Trying to reorganize your speech and shorten it to accommodate someone who is disorganized is not your job.

If your speaking time is 45 minutes, you know your formula is 10% of the time for the introduction, 85% of the time for the body, and 15% of the time for conclusion. You should know in advance whether your total time allotted includes time for questions. So, if you are slotted for 45 minutes and that includes questions from the audience, you need to allot time for that. You can't speak for 45 minutes and then take time for questions. You have to plan to allow for two to four questions or about 1 minute, 15 seconds per question and response. So, if you take two questions, you must allow 2 minutes, 30 seconds for questions, which allows only 42 minutes, 30 seconds for the speech.

The Use of Speaking Notes

There are many different points of view regarding the use of speech or presentation notes. Every expert has her own opinion on what works best and why. I advise my students and clients to use what makes them the most relaxed and comfortable.

There are pros and cons with every method, from writing out the entire speech or presentation to using no notes at all. Each person needs to use the approach that works best for him. While I am strongly opposed to a person reading a speech, if the presentation anxiety is so bad that it is debilitating and the speech or presentation has to be given, then reading may be the only option. In all other occasions, there are options each person can use that provide the opportunity to make eye contact with the audience, which is another step we cover next.

Example of Note Card Speaking Notes

The following is an example of a speaker's note card. The card shows key phrases for the presentation, self-reminder notes, and a safe word, and the cards are numbered to keep them in order:

[Smile]

Thank you. Welcome.

"No one wants their private and confidential medical records compromised... [pause]

But just about everyone would like to have them available to medial teams treating patients in emergency rooms, in operating rooms, in general practice, and for patients on demand as needed...in other words controlled by the patient! [Emphasis with hand]

> Today I would like to speak with you about the state of our—yours and mine—medical records.
>
> Specifically **What's in your medical records**? [SAFE WORD]
>
> Where are they? How many copies are there?
>
> Who has access to them and why? [pause...look concerned]
>
> Let's find out, and we will. [with confidence] [don't rock or pace]

As the speaker, your notes can be in whatever form you find most useful and convenient, including note cards—3x5 or 5x8, regular paper, typed, handwritten, graphic pictures, icons, or a combination of these. You have to decide what is best for you.

HANDOUTS

Do not give the audience anything during your speech or presentation. Doing so is deadly for the speaker. Handing out anything immediately divides the audience's attention and unintentionally sends them the *wrong signal* that the stuff on the handout as important as what you are saying. If you brought materials for the audience, hide it or have helpers hold it until your speech or presentation is completely over. Then announce handouts are available for the audience on their way out.

The Use of Audio Visual Aids

No part of public speaking arouses as much controversy and differences of opinion as the question of whether the speaker or presenter should use visual aids. There are basically two schools of thought on the use of visual aids as a support tool—use them or don't use them. This doesn't help you much, so let me see if I can make some sense of this. Before anyone can make an argument for or against the use of visual aids there has to be clarification of what kind of presentation they are to be used for.

To keep the discussion as simple as possible I divide all presentations into two types:

1. Speeches and presentations under an hour long

2. Lectures, seminars, workshops, conferences, and other events over an hour long

Obviously someone will come with a category that doesn't fit exactly into one of these two types. That's okay. If I divided them into three or four or ten types someone would still find fault with the approach, and it doesn't matter, so I will stick to the two.

My position is fairly simple. On the second type of presentations, seminar, workshop, and conference speakers who have an audience for hours as well as professors and instructors who have students for hours, and indeed for weeks, in an ongoing discussion of a topic or concepts have a need for visual cues to enhance their presentations. Sometimes models, formulas, theorems, positioning maps, marketing components, calculations, and other items are explained better with a visual representation accompanying the oral explanation. In these cases, visual aids, including PowerPoint presentations, are necessary and important to aid in the learning.

That said, most of the speeches and presentations for which I am offering these ten guidelines are the type that are under an hour in length and would not necessarily require PowerPoint, Prezi, or Haiku; whiteboards; overhead projectors; or flipcharts. However, in the unusual circumstance that for some reason they are absolutely necessary, here is a general rule that cannot lead you astray. If visual aids are used well they could possibly enhance a presentation by adding impact and strengthening audience involvement, yet if they are managed badly they can ruin a presentation completely.

My biggest concerns with the use of visual aids for short speeches and presentations are

- They add a layer of complexity and therefore additional anxiety to an already stressful situation, so why add to your anxiety with another variable where additional things could go wrong?

- In the type of speeches and presentations being discussed the presenters should be the center of attention not some visual aid. I do not think anything should subtract from the star of the performance—the speaker.

- It is like giving handouts during your speech or presentation. Once you put any visual aid up before an audience—whether it's a graphic or text or drawings on whiteboard or anything visual—their attention will go directly there. Some in the audience will remain fixated on the graphic and will be in constant anticipation of the next slide because they are the visual learners. Content placed on Power Point slides will be read and digested and begun to be analyzed by a great many in the audience before you are finished discussing the slide (explaining the content on the slide).

- Too many speakers and presenters get caught up in the technological capabilities of the software, and it's too easy to begin to add layers of animations, multiple transitions, blended colors, exotic shapes, and movement. Before long the presentation is a mess of shapes, colors, sizes, and transitions that distracts and fails to inform. The speaker's job is to inform; it's not the job of PowerPoint to inform or entertain.

An excellent PowerPoint presentation, "The Death of the PowerPoint," illustrates this problem well, and I recommend all my students and clients view it periodically. (See http://www.slideshare.net/thecroaker/death-by-powerpoint.)

I also recommend a funnier but just as powerful YouTube video by comedian Don McMillan titled "Life After Death by Power Point." As of January 6, 2015, the video had just over 1.8 million views. (Go to https://www.youtube.com/watch?v=KbSPPFYxx3o.)

- The type of visual aid you use cuts into the total time of your presentation leaving less time for you to speak, so you have to figure this in to your presentation timeline. It takes on average 2 to 3 minutes to clear a visual aid (explain it). Why give up control and surrender time to an inanimate device that can only rob you of time and sap the attention of your audience?

- It is too tempting for speakers and presenters to break eye contact with their audience and look back at the screen. I don't know why speakers do this, but it happens far too often. A speaker is delivering a presentation and has made good eye and emotional contact with his audience and in a second destroys the bond by turning his back on the audience to look at the screen. There perhaps is a fear among speakers that the Power Point bogeyman has somehow slipped in behind them and rearranged their slides or taken one out.

There is absolutely no reason for a speaker or presenter to look back at his slides. If you want to make reference to one particular bullet, number, phrase, word, or icon simply lift your arm and point backward in the general direction—the audience is smart enough to pick up what it is you want them to see.

If You Decide to Use Visual Aids

If you plan on using any slide software you should insist on using a good brand that offers good technical support and has a good reputation. PowerPoint has been on the market for more than 25 years and has maintained a solid reputation. Prezi has been on the market about six years and has worked to innovate its one whiteboard approach with a lot of motion. Haiku Deck is a relative newcomer but is suitable for speeches and presentations because it limits the amount of content per slide and emphasizes photos and graphics instead.

If you use PowerPoint slides, they should have roughly the following branding formula, which may sound a bit pedantic and narrow, but I go back to my original premise that slides and visual aids are not required or necessary and generally add a layer of complexity, risk, and anxiety. So if you are going to use visual aids you should have a set of guidelines that reduce the risk and anxiety as much as possible.

Creating and Building Your Slides

If you feel that you absolutely must have visual aids, there is a set of steps that need to be followed so that you reduce the risk of making mistakes and reduce the risk of adding to the tension already present in making a presentation.

- Use the exact same format for every slide—this means the same font. Choose an easily read font such as Courier, Arial, Arial Rounded Bold, or Times New Roman, and forget trying to get fancy with fonts that are based on scripts, italics, or other cursive characteristics that people are not used to and that are difficult to read. Think about your slides from the point of view of the person sitting in the chair farthest from the screen where the slide will be projected. What do the text and graphics look like from that person's seat?

- Change the font size only for titles and subtitles (if appropriate); otherwise, maintain the same font and type size throughout. We are striving for consistency and simplicity.

- Use left alignment for all titles, subtitles, and bullet points. This may not be the most attractive or creative approach to you, but think about how people read books, newspapers, text, and PowerPoint slides—left to right.

- Spell check and edit your slide copy. A speaker's credibility can be greatly diminished by a single spelling mistake or one graphic blooper. Have someone else style and spell check your slides.

- Style check every slide so that all bullets are the same style (that is, first letter capitalized, nouns capitalized, periods at the end or not, and so on). All slides must be standardized by style.

- Choose the slide (or visual aid) presentation color scheme theme—the background color and the font type color—and maintain this theme throughout the entire slide presentation. Again, we want consistency and simplicity.

There are nine different template outlines for PowerPoint presentations. For the short form presentation, if you use any PowerPoint slides at all, use the simplest template available and use the 4x4 bullet model. This is no more than four lines of text or bullets and no more than four words per line.

Haiku is another slide presentation program. This software offers graphic images and limited textual formats for simple presentations. Haiku may be better suited for the short form presentation if you feel slides are absolutely necessary. Most other presentation software is too sophisticated. For now, avoid anything else other than PowerPoint or Haiku.

A Word about the Color Scheme You Choose for Your Slides and Visual Aids

The color scheme you choose can help you make your slides and visual aids do their work of presenting information and supporting your speech or presentation. So, if you are going to use visual aids make them the most effective tools possible.

Color conveys meaning and influences people's attitudes. The colors you choose and the way you use them together can have a strong impact on your audience and how they receive your message.

Understanding the Relationship Between Colors

To help understand the influence of color let's begin with the color wheel. The color wheel contains 12 hues separated into three distinct groups:

1. The primary colors: red, blue, and yellow. In theory, all other colors can be derived from these three.

2. The secondary colors: green, violet, and orange. These are created by combining the primary colors.

3. The tertiary colors: red-orange, red-violet, blue-violet, blue-green, yellow-orange, and yellow-green. These are made from combinations of the first six colors.

Colors have specific relationships depending on their location on the color wheel. You can Google "Color Wheel" and use any example to see what a color wheel look like.

Colors opposite one another are called *complements,* and these colors contrast each other to create a *dynamic effect.*

Colors directly next to each other are called *analogous.* Each color has two analogous colors (one on each side of it). Analogous colors used together create a harmonious and unified feeling because two of the colors contain the third.

Color Selection Tips

As with the other components of your speech or presentation (that is, theme, main ideas, stories, and examples), when you choose your colors, you must consider your audience. Your goal is to strike a balance between professionalism and attractiveness. The following tips may help you choose the appropriate colors for your audience.

Color Combinations

- Save yourself time by using the predetermined color schemes in Microsoft PowerPoint, Prezi, Haiku, or other presentation software that successfully combines colors to format your presentations.

- Use colors sparingly for more effect and to avoid overwhelming the audience.

- According to some researchers, as many as 5% to 8% of men have some form of color blindness, red-green being the most common. For this reason, it's a good idea to limit the use of red and green to high contrast color combinations.

- Avoid relying exclusively on color to present information; everyone, including blind and visually impaired individuals, should get all the information from your presentation.

- Avoid at all costs, the temptation to give in to your secret deep down desire to be a wallpaper or fashion dress designer. You are going for *simplicity, simplicity, simplicity.*

Background Color

As a guideline, pick a background color of white or pale blue or gray and maintain one color of text throughout. *Dark background colors are deadly; avoid them completely.*

Certain color combinations provide high contrast for ease of reading. For example, the following combinations of text color on background color work well. Stick with these:

- Black or dark gray font on white background

- Dark blue font on white background

- Dark purple font on white background

- Dark red font on white background

- Black or dark gray font on pale blue or pale grey background

I think you sense a theme here. Why are books, magazines, and movie screens white? Because they are easier on the eye when viewers have to perceive subtle and direct images and text. While some people have found green on purple, violet on yellow, blue-green on red to be acceptable combinations, I don't like them because they violates the most basic guideline of simplicity.

When using graphics in your presentation, choose one color from the graphic to use as the text color. The color combinations will tie the elements of your slides together for a uniform look.

NOTE

Do not change the font or background color scheme. Once the color scheme has been selected for a PowerPoint slide presentation, do not change anything in the color scheme.

Color combinations frequently look different when projected, especially from different model projectors. Make every effort to test your presentation on the projector that will be used during your presentation to verify that the colors work well together. This allows you to make changes before the presentation, if necessary.

Using Your Slides

One of the drawbacks of using visuals, particularly slides, is that you *have to* use them. The point I am making is that having a graphic requires it to be shown, which requires time away from you the presenter and time to present the graphic to the audience. Too many things can go wrong when a graphic is added to the mix. The following to do list is designed to reduce the chances of a slide foul-up:

- Insist on changing your own slides. It is difficult and stress inducing to try to coordinate the slide changing with another person who does not know your speaking cadence or where you may add an ad lib or drop out a word or phrase, thus creating havoc with the slide transition. So borrow (better to buy your own) wireless digital slide changer for about $23 and practice your speech or presentation with you changing the slides.

- You want to do at least six full run-through dress rehearsals of your presentation with slides before the actual presentation. You will practice portions of the presentation many times, working on pace, cadence, pauses, tone, eye contact, and other aspects of your presentation.

  However, you will need to tie in the visual aids so they are seamless to you and the audience. The last thing you want is a break between a powerful statement and some visual aid. And the audience doesn't want nor deserve to hear something like. "Gee, I hope this slide works."

- Count on it taking 2 to 3 minutes to finish discussing each slide or what we call "clearing the slide." The reason for this is if you put up a slide with all the bullet points of the slide topic at once, you will need to go through and immediately "clear the slide," meaning quickly go down the list and mention what you are going to tell them (introduction), then go back and tackle each point (tell them), and quickly summarize the slide before moving on (tell them what you told them).

  One approach is to fly the topic points in one at a time thus the audience does not have the opportunity to read ahead of you. This is the best tactic if you insist on using slides. With 2 to 3 minutes to clear each slide, you know that if you have been given 45 minutes to speak you can't include more than 15 slides without it appearing as though you have just brought in an old-fashioned kaleidoscope viewer.

- Bring a copy of your PowerPoint presentation on a flash drive. Even if you are using your own laptop or iPad with the Power-Point in a file, bring a copy on a flash drive as a backup.

PowerPoint slides, as all visual aids, are merely support. They are a bit like players supporting your role as the star performer and as such need to be in the background. Simplicity is what you are going for. Audiences are want uniformity and comfort in viewing visual aids. This means comfortable colors, brief text, and clear graphics (if you use any).

Drawing on Whiteboards and Flipcharts

The use of whiteboards and flipcharts is simply not practical for most speeches and presentations. While they may work for workshops and training, for a speech or presentation with limited time, it just takes too long to draw an illustration or write a statement on a whiteboard or flipchart. Total presentation time would be severely limited, not to mention your back would be to your audience for a great deal of time.

Audio and Video and Web Content

Audio and video devices and web content are excellent for certain types of training, workshops, and educational content delivery but are generally not good for brief speeches and presentations. The broadband issues, graphics uncertainties, slow loading, sound quality issues, and any number of technological issues make these formats too risky to use in the short time allowed for a speech or presentation. The very nature of the technological issues involved adds layers of complexity, including the need for additional equipment and support staff, all of which is avoidable risk.

Overhead Projectors (OHP)

While not quite as limiting as whiteboards and audio and video devices, overhead projectors can still create a logistics problem. Slides can be prepared on acetates, both in written and graphic form, ahead of time, but to mark them up or make additions or edits the speaker must have the marking pencil, liquid cleaner, and a cloth. OHP slides do command attention, but care must be taken to keep the audience's attention on the slides while the speaker focuses her attention on the audience.

Key Takeaways

- Prepare early and often—don't wait.

- Take advantage of your unconscious brain's attempt to help.

- Focus on answering six questions—What, When, Where, Why, How, and Who—and almost any speech or presentation will be a success.

- Determine what you want your audience to take away from your remarks. Usually you can make three or four points that will be remembered by the audience.

- Know something about your audience.

- Every speech or presentation is really a conversation with a few friends and should have three distinct parts: introduction, main body, and conclusion.

- Never give an audience handouts during a presentation.

4

Step 4: Walk with Purpose to the Podium; Smile, Pause, Then Smile, Smile, Smile

---

We shall never know all the good that a smile will do.

—**Mother Theresa**

You may have heard that first impressions count and last a lifetime. Well, they do! In a previous book I wrote on personal networking titled Networking for Recent College Graduates, I discussed research that has been conducted on first impressions and body language. One of the most striking findings is that in less than a second people form lifelong impressions (good or bad) of us based on their first contact or first viewing of us. The research went on to show that most of what is perceived in these initial micro observations takes place by visual and nonverbal cues or in other words, before an understandable word is spoken.

As we mentioned earlier in the book, 93% of human communication is nonverbal—through body language. This means in your speech or presentation—or hopefully your conversation with your audience—the vast majority of what you communicate will not be in what you say, but in how your audience visually perceives you initially, how you say what you are going to say, and then how you use your body.

Amy Cuddy's 2012 presentation "Your Body Language Shapes Who You Are," is the second most-viewed TED talk ever, with 19 million views to date (http://www.youtube.com/watch?v=Ks-_Mh1QhMc). Knowing the importance of first impressions gives you two advantages that you should be aware of and then be prepared to use to your advantage. If you know your audience is going to be making micro judgments about you, you can effectively manage how you are going to be perceived by carefully choreographing your first appearance (your first impression) and your approach to the podium.

You manage this perception by what you are wearing, your grooming, your bearing, your stance, how you hold yourself, and your walk or stride to your speaking space. The confidence you exude creates a strong positive initial impression. The second benefit of doing this is so you can actually change the way you feel about yourself. Not only does the audience feel a powerful positive energy toward you, but you feel more confident within.

Your Speaking Space

A podium, for our purposes, is any device that raises a platform or shelf above normal desk or table height for the purposes of providing a place for a speaker or presenter to rest his notes or materials related to his presentation. Podiums go by several commonly used names, including podia, lecterns, daises, plinths, platforms, pedestals, public speaking stands, rostrums, and pulpits. Podiums normally come in wood, plastic, or metal.

Podiums are designed and built for providing speakers and presenters with a place to hold notes, materials necessary for a presentation, and perhaps a place to rest their hands. While in some cases there may be a limited amount of space for a laptop or iPad, I recommend never attempting to give a speech or presentation with an electronic or digital device on the podium top shelf. This is not what they are designed for, and speakers and presenters risk unnecessary problems and distractions with these devices in full view of the audience. Furthermore, electronic devices are difficult to read, subject to failure, and present many potential problems a speaker does not need.

In many cases, with enough advance notice, the speaker can request and receive information on what kind of podium and speaking space is available. Speakers have every right to request the equipment (for example, podium, lighting, side tables, slide changer, and microphone—either on the podium, handheld, or portable belt pack) she needs.

Standing at the podium, on a platform, or anywhere in front of an audience, you should be balanced on both feet, with feet shoulder width apart, one foot slightly in front of the other (usually the one closer to the audience in front), and at a slight angle to the audience. Avoid putting more weight on one leg or foot or shifting your weight back and forth (see Figure 4.1). This is called the *ready position*.

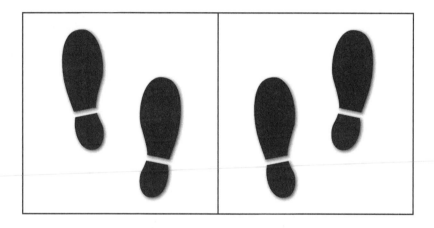

Figure 4.1 The ready position (either left or right foot slightly forward)

Your arms should hang naturally at your sides unless you are gesturing, which is okay as long as you do it below shoulder level. When gesturing, try to avoid pointing a finger or using a fist. These gestures need to be carefully controlled or they come across in body language as negative in tone. There are places and times to use such gestures, but it isn't likely a novice speaker would be in a position to do so.

Your walk to where you will speak is critical because it is the last thing the audience sees before you begin to speak. Your walk should not be too quick or a slow amble, but a purposeful stride with shoulders back, chin up, and, of course, a big smile on your face.

Prior to Your Speech or Presentation

There is a ritual found in the theater, athletics, and other professions called the *walk-through*. This is part of the preparation and consists of arriving early and walking through the grounds, arena, field of play, or stage where you will be performing, presenting, or speaking.

The point is you want to have been there before so when you arrive to speak it's not the first time you see everything. This cuts down on anxiety and fear. You get some sense of the layout and your arena. You get some sense of the sound equipment, acoustics, temperature, lighting, position of the podium, microphone, distance from where you will be sitting to the podium—the whole layout.

Take an opportunity to stand at the podium and speak a few sentences to get comfortable with your position. If possible, take a run-through with your presentation and graphics, if you use any, with the equipment. If possible, leave your notes on the podium so you don't have to carry them with you as you stride to the podium when announced.

Your Speaking Preparation

With this knowledge, you need to practice walking—striding—to the place where you will deliver your remarks. Your walk should be purposeful, with shoulders back, head up, (swagger a little if you feel like it), smiling, and confident.

When you get to the place where you are going to speak, stop. Take a breath and smile as you look out into the audience. I use something I call the three section model. Divide the room into three sections, and as you glance into each section, see whether you can pick out a set of eyes or a smiling face that you can connect with instantly. Register that person's location because you are going to go back to that person throughout your remarks.

This nonverbal communication has begun to connect the audience to you, and most people in the audience have hopefully begun to form favorable images of you even before you have said a word. Some speakers are so nervous they begin speaking as they are walking to the podium or immediately upon arrival at the podium. Fight that urge. Take a moment, smile, and look around.

Never tap or blow into the microphone with a comment such as, "does this thing work?" Such behavior is amateurish and destroys the buildup and first impression you have worked to produce with your nonverbal cues. If the first words out of your mouth make you sound like you don't belong in front of an audience that is what the audience will think. You do not want them to think that or you will have an uphill road in your speech or presentation.

Speaker's Insurance

I have a speaker's kit that I preposition at the podium at the walk-through should I need anything during the presentation:

- A small flashlight to have in the event the podium light fails or is not bright enough
- A glass of water in case the organization forgets to provide one
- A couple of spare batteries for each electronic component you carry
- A spare remote wireless slide changer
- A spare copy of a written outline of your speech and a felt-tip pen
- A couple of small versatile heavy-duty clips or clamps

- A handkerchief

- A small package of lozenges (open)

Key Takeaways

- Smile from start to finish.

- Be aware of your position at the podium and your posture.

- Make sure you arrive early and have time to do a complete and thorough walk-through.

- Test the microphone so you don't have to test it just before you begin your remarks.

- Stride confidently to your speaking space and pause to smile before you begin your remarks.

- Make eye contact with the audience.

5

Step 5: Make and Keep Eye Contact with the Audience

Eye contact is way more intimate than words will ever be.

—**Faraaz Kazi**

A critical point about body language for speakers and presenters is how people judge our honesty and sincerity by our willingness to hold eye contact an appropriate amount of time. In a one-on-one conversation experts believe that holding eye contact for 7 to 10 seconds before breaking it off briefly and then regaining eye contact is normal and a sign the person is not hiding anything or lying. In one-on-one conversations avoiding eye contact is seen as a negative sign, as is holding eye contact for too long a period of time, which can be creepy and ominous.

In front of an audience the eye contact rule is slightly different since a speaker doesn't normally look at a single person but the entire audience. The audience expectation is the speaker should keep eye contact and prove her sincerity and credibility. When speaking, unless the speaker has notes, there should be constant eye contact with the audience. However, the speaker should avoid blank or bland staring into one section of the audience for the entire speech, which is why I recommend the three section model.

Figure 5.1 is a graphic of an audience chamber and shows a three-part eye contact model. Dividing the room into sections A, B, and C gives the speaker a plan for moving his eyes in a pattern rather than randomly scanning or moving indiscriminately around the room.

The speaker makes eye contact with section A of the room and depending on the speaker's skill and poise she may pick out one or two audience members who have reciprocal smiles or otherwise seem to connect with the speaker. Then the speaker can choose to move to section B, and then C.

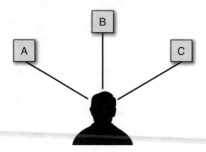

Figure 5.1 Dividing the audience chamber into three sections

The speaker makes and holds eye contact with an individual or with the section. Eye contact with the section is simply accomplished by looking slightly above the foreheads of the people in the center of the section. The speaker should hold eye contact until a sentence or phrase is completely finished and then the eye contact can be shifted to another person or another section. It is important to hold eye contact completely through the sentence or phrase before shifting; otherwise, the speaker gives off nonverbal body language of a shifty, untrustworthy person.

As tempting as it may be to keep going back to the friendliest faces, make every effort to move your eye contact around the room as evenly as possibly. Moving your eye contact around the room provides the entire audience evidence that you are talking to everyone in the room.

Of course if you use notes, you will have to break eye contact to refer to your notes. However, if you have practiced you presentation at least six times, you will be able to quickly glance at your notes, find what you need, and regain eye contact with the audience as quickly as possible.

NOTE

Do not shift eye contact until you have finished a complete thought or sentence. When you have finished the thought or sentence, then shift your eyes. The speaker seems less focused and sincere when she is speaking while moving her eyes.

For speakers or presenters who really struggle with stage fright, remember the three smiling faces identified when you first walked to your speaking position. Any time you feel flustered, need support, or feel awkward, shift your eyes to one of those three faces and reenergize. Remember they want you to succeed.

The Use of PowerPoint and Other Graphics

There is a great temptation for speakers and presenters to glance back, or worse, look away from their audience to look at a PowerPoint slide or graphic. If you break eye contact with your audience you are basically saying, "You folks are no longer important, but this slide is so I am going to look at it."

If you have rehearsed your presentation and prepared your PowerPoint presentation you know the order of the slides. Who would have changed them? Why do you need to look at the slide and lose eye contact with the audience? There is no reason. If you need to refer to something on the slide, simply mention it. The audience can see it, so you don't have to point to it.

Key Takeaways

- Make and keep eye contact with the audience.

- Speakers should speak or appear to be speaking to the entire audience.

- Hold eye contact with the person you have established it with until you have completed a full sentence or phrase. Then you can shift to another person, but do not shift eye contact as you are talking because it makes you looks shifty and insincere.

- Divide the audience chamber into at least three sections and move eye contact from section to section rather than randomly scanning or moving your gaze indiscriminately around the room.

6

Step 6: Take Control of Your Speaking Space and Your Speaking

Remember not only to say the right thing in the right place, but far more difficult still, to leave unsaid the wrong thing at the tempting moment.

—Benjamin Franklin

As you wait for your introduction to be complete, you have a minute or two to loosen up and make your final preparations for your remarks. If you are in view of the audience make sure you are smiling. Try to inconspicuously tighten and loosen major muscle groups (that is, legs, trunk, back). This isometric exercise routine has been used by athletes and performers for years to help them loosen up just prior to a performance. The last thing, just before you step to the podium, take one or two deep breaths, breathing in through your nose and out through your mouth. Try breathing from the diaphragm and not the chest.

Once you are introduced and walk to your speaking space you are in command of the speech or presentation. You are the captain of the ship. The oldest military metaphors apply: Take control of the high ground and the center, and you are in a commanding position.

The speaking space is your space; it's your high center ground. Just as in military strategy when the high ground is an advantage or as in a game of chess, you control the movement of all the pieces and decide how things go. In your preliminary walk-through you should have checked the sound, room temperature, lights, and equipment. Unless something highly unusual like an electrical failure occurs, everything should function as you practiced.

On a prearranged signal the lights and other electrical equipment should be in the go position, and you are ready to take your position.

Be a Leader

Once you are introduced and take your speaking space, you assume the role of conditional leader of the speech or presentation. The audience will follow your lead as long as they are inspired, entertained, intellectually rewarded, informed, engaged, or whatever your remarks have promised them. They expect you to perform and be in control of the situation (again they are always thankful it's not them).

Being in control does not mean asserting power; it means having influence. There is an important difference. Having or asserting power carries with it the use of or the threat of the use of force, coercion, intimidation, or fear to get others to do what you want. Force is an impractical, inefficient, short-term tool because it requires the constant application of ever increasing levels of force. Influence, on the other hand is a more effective, more efficient tool because it gets people to do what you want by engaging them in common goals because they benefit as well.

The audience expects a benefit from listening, and as the leader of the speaking session, you have to make sure you properly articulate what that benefit is. There are ways you demonstrate leadership, including

- Your first impression.
- The way you handle unusual situations, such as the visual arts not working, the room lights failing, heating or cooling malfunctioning, the sound system failing, audience members arriving late or leaving early, too few seats, your program inadvertently starting late, or any number of situations not under the speaker's control.

NOTE

The responsibility of the speaker is to deliver the promised remarks and the rewards of those remarks.

THE SHOW MUST GO ON

It would take another book to provide just my own personal examples of unusual situations that have occurred during speaking engagements. But it might be helpful to give a few examples to demonstrate the speaker's main responsibility, which is you have to find a way to deliver your remarks.

I once was a keynote speaker at a conference, which featured several hundred business executives from the telemarketing industry. I had just begun an important speech on recent legislative issues impacting the industry when a fire alarm for the entire convention center went off. As we began to evacuate, the hotel manager notified us that it was a false alarm. Shortly after, the fire marshal informed us that it was a remote digital malfunction, and it would take up to an hour to shut off the alarm, which could be turned down to a low annoying constant ring. With no danger to the attendees, I asked what they wanted to do, and they overwhelmingly voted that they wanted to hear the keynote. So I cranked up the microphone and spoke over the alarm for 50 minutes.

Another example of the show must go on occurred back in pre-Power-Point days when speakers used glass and plastic slides. I was presenting immediately before the main speaker who was just about to hand three trays of slides to the projectionist, when he tripped and dumped about 300 slides on the floor. In the mad rush to reassemble the slides in their proper order, it was obvious to me it was going to take about 10 to 15 minutes. The conference promoter signaled me to stretch out my remarks to 15 more minutes. I was just ready to move to my conclusion and had to shift gears and speak another 15 minutes.

Hopefully these kinds of situations will never happen to you. The point is that you can't prepare for the unknown, but you have to have the leadership to manage the situation. The audience expects it.

- The way you handle the audience. This includes setting ground rules like no questions during the presentation and maintaining a professional demeanor with any rude audience member. It's rare, but occasionally an audience member, usually in an attempt to show off, acts inappropriately. As a speaker, you always must maintain your cool and project a calm demeanor.

NOTE

Never, ever lose it in front of an audience. Regardless of the situation, you will always leave a bad impression.

- The way you begin and end your remarks. We discuss this more in Chapter 9, "Step 9: The Last Thing You Do Is What Most People Will Remember—Do It Well," but the way you conclude your presentation is how many will remember you, so get that step right.
- Your use of rhetorical techniques.
- Your smile.
- Your confidence.
- Your passion.
- The way you handle interruptions (for example, cell phones, alarms, people coming and going).

Rules of the Speaking Space

Public speaking is a combination of what is said and the visual actions taken by the speaker. The success or failure of a speech or presentation is determined as much by what is said as by how it is said and all the nonverbal cues that take place in between the words. It all has to be choreographed into a seamless event.

Don't Dance with the Podium, Lean on It, Use It for a Drum, or Strangle It

The podium can be an icon of the great orator. It can symbolize memorable moments when men and women made history with words. It can be a place for speakers to keep their notes hidden from the audience. The podium can be many useful things. But when it is used for something other than communicating an idea, it can be a hindrance or even a barrier between the speaker and the audience—the last thing a speaker wants.

For many people the podium offers some comfort from stage fright. It's something to hold onto and to help them to stop shaking. This support is okay as long as the shaking doesn't get so bad you start shaking the whole podium and it appears as though you and the podium are dancing the samba.

Another downside of grasping the podium too hard is you can cut off the blood supply to your hands, causing your hands to go limp, which is not good.

A bad podium move is to lean on it. Some people unconsciously first rest their wrists, then their forearms, then their arms, and finally they are leaning forward like they are preparing to dive into a swimming pool.

Avoid grasping the podium and either patting or drumming the fingers on the sides. Not only is this visually distracting, but if the podium has a microphone the noise can get very loud.

The proper stance behind a podium is to have either one or both hands loosely resting on the sides of the podium or either one or both hands relaxed on the podium slanted shelf or neither hands on the podium but rather resting at the speaker's side.

To Use or Not to Use a Microphone

If the podium has a microphone on a stand, you should have adjusted it to your best position during the walk-through before your speech. You do not want to be talking directly into a microphone or talking up to one. The ideal position is to have your mouth about 2 to 4 inches above the microphone and to talk over the top of it.

Never ever blow into or tap the microphone to see whether it is working. If you checked it during the walk-through, it will be okay for the presentation.

If the microphone is fixed, remember as you turn your head you will lose volume, so you will either have to adjust your volume or lean closer to the microphone for those moments. The best speaking technique when a microphone is used is to never speak while your face is turned away from the microphone. As you move eye contact around the room shift your shoulders slightly so you are facing that person or section.

If the microphone is a handheld type, your speaking job just became a little more complex. With a handheld microphone you have to manually hold the device in such a manner that you don't touch anything and don't lose volume. Also, if you clap with the audience, set the microphone down or hold it under one arm. Don't clap with a microphone in one hand because it sounds like thunder.

If at all possible, you want to avoid the handheld microphone. If you have made arrangements with the event planner early enough, you should be able to request and ensure that if a microphone is needed it is attached to the podium.

Depending on the size of the audience chamber and the number of people in the audience, you may decide a microphone is or is not necessary. Remember the person in the farthest row and farthest seat must be able to hear you in your normal tone.

Wearing and Holding Eyeglasses

The question arises frequently as to whether a speaker or presenter should wear eyeglasses when giving a speech or presentation. There is no one easy answer that fits all situations. Generally my response is unless the situation requires you to read your speech or presentation (in cases of extreme performance anxiety) or read names such as honorees or recipients and you absolutely need your eyeglasses for this, then don't wear them.

I've seen too many polished speakers fall into a bad nervous habit of repeatedly taking their eyeglasses on and off throughout their remarks. First, in my opinion, eyeglasses are a barrier between your eyes and the eyes of your audience. Clear lenses or not, they form a barrier.

If the speaker succumbs to the nervous tick of taking the glasses on and off repeatedly, it becomes a distraction. It can even become one of several different types of distractions in which some audience members may begin to count the number of times the speaker removes her glasses and even begins to anticipate when this will occur. This turns the audience's attention away from what is really being said.

The second possible outcome of removing one's eyeglasses is they can become something held in the speaker's or presenter's hand—something we don't want to have happen.

You Don't Need to Hold on to Distractions While Speaking

Objects held in the speaker's or presenter's hand such as glasses, pointers, pens, pencils, iPhones, books, keys, jewelry, or anything else can become a distraction or, worse, an unintentional projectile. I have seen speakers mark themselves in the face with grease pencils, ink pens, magic markers, and pencils. I have seen speakers twirl their eyeglasses by the earpiece and lose control, flinging the eyeglasses across the stage, striking themselves in the head, or, worse, letting the glasses fly into the audience. I have seen speakers unintentionally fling sets of car keys, iPhones, magic markers, even textbooks across the stage and into the audience.

Laser pointers are another possible nuisance and should not be held. I have seen speakers unintentionally advance slides not knowing they had their fingers on the forward or reverse button. Even worse, I have seen speakers waving their handheld remote slide changer laser beams into the audience chamber.

Never Hold Up Anything from the Podium

A speaker or presenter using a podium should not have anything to show the audience from the podium. Most people in the audience have a normal range of vision, and even those with better than 20/20 vision will not be able to see anything you hold up, so why do it? Holding up things is amateurish, awkward, and risky; there is no good reason to do it.

If you are giving an award, it should be placed behind the podium or more properly on a separate table.

Control the Pace of the Presentation

Once you begin your remarks you are in command of the bridge; you control what happens for the next period of time assigned for the speaking session. You know the total amount of time allotted to your remarks.

You know whether a question and answer period will follow. You know it takes 2 to 3 minutes to clear any audio visual aid. You know nervousness and adrenaline will cause you to speed up your normal speaking pace. These issues have to be factored in to controlling the pace so that you conclude on time.

Unknown events beyond your control might happen and affect the pace or length of your presentation. In spite of all the planning and prechecking during the walk-through it is possible (Murphy's Law) something could go wrong. The trick is adapting to the situation and not allowing hiccups to rob you of the control you've established.

Don't Stand in the Light of the Projector

If you use an overhead projector or a projector in the rear of the room, make a point to avoid standing in the light beam of the projector. The light beam makes you squint your eyes, and the projection of the images on your face gives you the appearance of an Andy Warhol poster.

Use Positive Style Whenever Possible

Your audience will listen to your words, your body language, and how you say what you say. Their visual, audio, and psychological senses will want to put all this together to come away with some kind of feeling about you, and a positive feeling is best. If you speak with passion and commitment, use active words, especially power verbs, take a positive approach, offer possible answers to questions and solutions to problems. Your audience will come away from your speech or presentation feeling that your remarks had a positive style, and they will be uplifted.

Avoid the Negative

No matter the situation; no matter that it may seem like the ideal opportunity to speak up concerning certain contemporary events, news, or situations; no matter what others do or say; no matter what—do not get negative under any circumstances.

It could be tempting, especially if you sense the audience is enthusiastically behind something or is riled up about something. You might be tempted to earn the crowd's approval by helping to be their voice. Resist this urge. You are not there to cheerlead a mob or incite a riot. You have a job as a speaker for the topic you have selected. You have a leader's responsibility.

Likewise, if there are problems with the audio visual equipment, power, lights, or any number of things, you have to show poise, control, and leadership.

You should try to avoid speaking about certain topics anyway, such as politics, religion, ethics, morality, parenting, and social issues. These generate strong feelings and can divide an otherwise natural audience. Focus on the positive.

Know When to Be Silent

By being silent I am not referring to the use of the pause. I am referring to holding your comments if there is applause. When the audience appreciates a point you have made, they can show their appreciation by applauding. Don't be in a hurry to rush on with your remarks. Hold until the applause is over and then continue.

If You Don't Smile You Leave It Up to the Audience to Figure Out What's on Your Mind

I have discussed how much of human communication is nonverbal and therefore how important the smile and first impression are. So, if you are the speaker or presenter and you don't smile, the audience will have to search for visual cues as to who are you. Your face will be their first target. If you don't smile and that is what they see, what do you believe they will think?

Don't Wear Your Watch

While this goes for most jewelry, it is especially true with a watch. The reason for not wearing a watch is anyone can have a nervous moment and what do we do in a nervous moment? We do some kind of comfortable gesture such as look at our watch. It may be just a nervous gesture to you, but to the audience it says, "I'm so bored when will this be over?" This is not the nonverbal signal you want to send.

If you need a timepiece to keep track of the speaking time, take off your watch and place it on the podium where you can glance at it without the audience thinking you have a better place to be.

Understand the Impact of Your Nonverbal Communications

Remember the importance of body language and how much of your communication is going to be transmitted through nonverbal signals. People in all cultures use gestures spontaneously when speaking. An audience will gain little from the words alone if a speaker merely stands up and speaks with little body movement. Gestures enhance the message if done properly. When gestures support the message, they enhance your communication; however, when they don't, gestures are just distracting and can confuse the audience.

A single or occasional gesture is mostly insignificant; however, repeated and constant gestures become signals that either confirm or contradict what is being said. At the same time, if you don't use any gestures at all, you appear stiff and uncomfortable. Or if your arms flail about you seem scattered and silly.

Numerous books deal with the topic of body language and go into great detail about the various meanings ascribed to different gestures. One could devote an enormous amount of time to the topic. If such depth of knowledge were practical for our purposes, I would include more on the topic. I have tried to summarize what a speaker or presenter needs to know without adding anxiety about learning more things. I have tried to limit the information to what can be managed in a short time frame and provide a basic foundation. If the subject interests you, by all means pursue it further on your own because it will make you a more effective communicator.

Stay Inside the Box

Try to imagine you have something like that digital strike zone super-imposed on batters when baseball games are broadcast on television. Computer animation is used to create a box (the strike zone) for viewers to see where the pitcher's various pitches are coming at the batter.

As a speaker you have an imaginary zone that begins at your waist extends up to your neck and out to an area approximately a few inches outside shoulder width. This is your "gesture zone." Like a baseball batter's strike zone, sometimes you will go outside the zone on purpose for some intended effect, but the zone is where you want to be most of time. Your hands should be kept open (unless you are trying for a special effect with a fist) and palms exposed in an outward and upward position.

If a speaker's hands repeatedly extend outside the box, especially above the shoulder or head, it can be interpreted as though the speaker is erratic, unpredictable, and even fitful.

If a speaker repeatedly covers or touches his face, the body language signals are generally negative. The audience receives a nonverbal signal that the speaker is not being truthful, is hiding something, or may lack credibility or honesty.

Here are the meanings of some other common gestures:

- Repeatedly touching the nose is called the Pinocchio effect and could signal that the speaker is lying.

- Hands or fingers that repeatedly come up and swipe, touch, or cover the lips or mouth have a negative signal of a person trying to hold back the truth.

- Hands tugging or pulling at or scratching the ear or ears sends the signal that you really don't want to hear this.

- Hands holding, grasping, stroking, tapping the side of the head, or rubbing the eyes are signals that the speaker is in pain over this and wishes it was over.

- Steepling or interlocking the fingers in front of the face is a blocking or holding back signal.

- Palms outward at face level is a signal that the speaker is holding the audience back, unconsciously telling them to stay away.

- Wrinkling the forehead and narrowing or squinting the eyes are signals of boredom or being in pain.

- Raising one or both eyebrows shows skepticism.

- The chin down is a sign of a defense posture or lack of self-confidence.

- Widened eyes with lips drawn tight is a sign of anger.

- Pulling on one's collar is a signal of nervous dread or "the heat is on; I can't wait to escape."

Other Nonverbal Signals Around the Body

Generally hand and arm gestures below the waist are just plain odd and should be avoided by a speaker. A speaker's hand and arm gestures made with the palm up are considered more warm and friendly, while gestures made with the palms down are considered more firm or ominous. The same applies to the fist. If a speaker wants to make a strong emphasis on a point, the fist can be stuck into the other palm or in a shallow downward motion from the shoulder several inches. This is effective used sparingly. Used too frequently and the message is negative.

Pointing is an aggressive signal, and the double finger point doubles the aggression. The speaker should avoid pointing directly at the audience. Instead the pointing finger or fingers should be aimed upward or outward to some distant point. Politicians are often guilty of the aggressive point, which I call the "dragon slayer" gesture.

Keep your hands out of your pockets. There is no situation in which a speaker looks professional with his hands in his pocket or pockets. Hands on the hips or arms folded in front are negative signals. Typically they are guarding or power signals depending on the situation. A nervous speaker might use either of the gestures, but it still signals guarding and that is not the message to send to an audience.

A speaker should avoid turning her head or head and body so that it appears she is giving the "side or downward glance," which is a negative signal. In a normal two-person conversation, the side glance is a negative message that says I distrust you. If a speaker from a podium does it, the message is magnified.

It may seem odd to some to mention this, but it is necessary: Keep both feet flat on the floor. Some speakers exhibit their nervousness by some or all of the following: standing on one foot, crossing their legs (while standing), reaching down and grabbing one leg or foot, and even taking the yoga position of the "tree" with one leg bent and the foot resting on the other knee. These positions look awkward and are distracting to the audience. They also can cause speakers problems such as losing their balance or, worse, falling to the floor.

Slouching is not only poor posture it is a nonverbal signal of noninterest.

Positive Nonverbal Signs to Watch For

So far most of what I have been talking about with regards to nonverbal communications has dealt with what you as a speaker need to avoid signaling. Now, I want to shift gears a little and point out some of the positive signs you can watch for as well as use to send positive nonverbal signals. The same basic rule applies in that one signal is never enough to make a sound judgment. You need to see repeated use of the signal.

If during your eye contact with the audience you notice individuals leaning back in their chairs or from their waists you might initially interpret this as a negative gesture. However, if the leaning backward is combined with a slight turning of the chin exposing part of the neck, or the head tilted slightly to the right, this is considered a positive reaction. In animals it is the submissive gesture. In humans it shows vulnerability and openness.

Widened eyes with the mouth slightly open is a positive sign and generally signals approval, trust, and even vulnerability.

Smiling naturally is of course a signal of approval and acceptance. It is tough to fake this kind of smile, and we can generally pick up a fake smile. Variations of the smile are the quick flash smile or the faux smile and the slow smile—one that takes between .5 and 1 second to appear. The quick smile is less sincere.

The head nod (up and down) is a signal for approval and acknowledgment. You can begin this gesture, and in many cases if the audience is in agreement with your speech, you will receive reciprocal head nodding back from members of the audience.

If you are inclined to try something different you can test your audience as to whether they are in agreement with your talking points.

Scientists attribute these actions to human brain cells called *mirror neutrons,* also called "monkey see monkey do" cells. These unusual brain cells function only when we perform an action or when we see, hear, or even suspect another person is about to perform the very same action. These cells literally make us "feel" that action in our body.

Simple examples of this in action include yawning, laughing, crying, and blushing, which are contagious. You can see this at work if during your remarks you begin to nod your head in a positive motion. In just a few seconds, you should see several audience members mimicking you behavior. By the way, it works using the no head shake also, so don't do it that way.

Use a Simple Three-Part Approach

You probably have noticed that up to now there have been no ideas, suggestions, or clues that actually deal with public speaking. This is because there are two parts to becoming an adequate speaker. You have to understand the nonspeaking issues and manage those, and then learn a few speaking techniques.

Many books on how to become better speakers focus solely or primarily on the techniques of public speaking. These are written mostly for people who enjoy getting up in front of crowds and just want to improve their techniques and get better at speaking.

I've trained speakers, gone to speakers school, read about and seen firsthand most of the techniques of public speaking, and I haven't found one that is better than the three step-model for a speech, which is the introduction, body, and conclusion.

This model simply takes every speaking situation and divides it into three parts:

- The introduction, which should take about 15% of your total allotted time.

- The body, which should take about 75% of your total allotted time.

- The conclusion, which should take about 10% of your total allotted time.

The introduction is your opportunity to let the audience know what your presentation is going to be about. You can use quotes, jokes, current articles, facts, figures, graphics—anything that gets the attention of the audience—but be careful when using humor.

The body is the main part of your remarks. The body of your presentation or speech is where you present the two to three key points you want the audience to take away and remember. The purpose of limiting the number of points to two or three is this is the limit of an audience's tolerance. Most people will not be able to recall more than two or three main points, so why prepare and deliver more?

The conclusion is your wrap-up of what you covered in the body. Only cover what you mentioned in the body. If you forget or left out something in the body, do not mention it in the conclusion.

You should develop a transition sentence that takes you from the introduction to the body and from the body to the conclusion.

Most People Will Only Remember Two to Three Things You Said

Follow George Orwell's five rules of a good communicator:

1. Never use a metaphor, simile, or other figure of speech that you are used to seeing in print. Examples: toe the line, stand shoulder to shoulder with, no axe to grind.

2. Never use a long word where a short one will do.

3. If it is possible to cut a word out, always cut it out.

4. Never use the passive where you can use the active.

5. Never use a foreign phrase, scientific word, or jargon if you can think of an everyday English equivalent.

And a final word of advice: Finish on time (or a little ahead if possible).

Key Takeaways

- The speaker controls the speaking space and is the leader of the event.

- The audience will make a split-second micro judgment—a first impression—of you as you walk to the speaking space. You have a powerful influence on this impression by your demeanor, grooming, and stance.

- Both you and the audience will be sending and receiving non-verbal body language signals during the presentation. Both you and the audience will be trying to justify your impressions and interpretations by the nonverbal body signals.

- As the speaker, you have control of the verbal and nonverbal signals and therefore the complete communications message going out to the audience.

- Use a speaking style that accentuates positive words and avoid a negative approach.

- Make sure you finish on time.

7

Step 7: You'll Make Mistakes— Don't Apologize, Just Keep Going

Anyone who has never made a mistake has never tried anything new.

—Albert Einstein

Very few speeches and presentations are perfect. Even with speeches prepared far in advance and practiced over and over again, mistakes can be made. The most professional and most polished speakers and entertainers make mistakes all the time. Unless you are singing the national anthem and forget the words, or make up new lyrics as a number of performers have done, the audience has no idea you made a mistake.

Most of the time when you give a speech or a presentation the audience does not have a prepared copy of your remarks. Therefore they have no idea know what you are going say or when you are going to say it.

NOTE

If you make a mistake, ignore it; do not apologize and just keep going with your remarks. Even if you think the mistake is a whopper, the audience is not likely to know, so *do not stop and call their attention to it.* Believe me, the vast majority of people will not catch a mistake unless you call their attention to it.

One of the greatest orators of all time was Dr. Martin Luther King, Jr., and his finest moment was the "I Have a Dream" speech on the National Mall in August 1963. The speech had been examined and reviewed by many experts, and an important point has come to light. Dr. King departed from his carefully prepared notes on two occasions and ad libbed the now famous anaphoric "I have a dream" portions. The hundreds of thousands of spectators did not know the speech had been altered from the prepared text; only a handful of close associates knew.

Many entertainers, professors, ministers, politicians, and speakers of all types have made mistakes but keep going forward. The two oldest adages in show business are never let them see you sweat and the show must go on.

I classify mistakes into two categories: Mistakes of planning and mistakes of performance.

Mistakes of planning are things that go wrong because of poor planning These are mistakes for which the speaker is responsible and are completely correctable if another speaking opportunity comes along. Some mistakes of planning include the following:

- **Not having the right message for the audience**—This is simply the result of not probing the person who extended the invitation and asking questions about who the audience will be made up of.

- **Not practicing enough**—This is the result of, for whatever reason(s), not devoting the time to rehearsing the complete speech a minimum of six times.

- **Lacking preparation or focus**—This is a result of not spending enough time doing research on the speaking topic or not understanding the topic or its connection or relevance to the audience.

- **Speaking for too long**—This is the result of, for whatever reason(s), not devoting the time to rehearsing the complete speech a minimum of six times and practicing to stay within the allotted time.

- **Projecting the wrong brand/image**—This is a result of failing to understand the speaker's control of the important first impression and the follow-up nonverbal cues that send positive signals.

- **Using visual aids inappropriately**—This is caused by deciding to use visual aids when they should have been avoided. Also, it can result from lack of full rehearsal practice with the visual aids and the remarks together.

- **Making mistakes during the presentation that could have been prevented with a walk-through**—This is an almost totally avoidable mistake. A preliminary presentation walk-through, including a microphone sound check, light check, heating and cooling check, audio visual equipment check, stage check, and voice test prevents a multitude of problems from occurring during the presentation.

- **Showing up late**—Aside from a medical emergency I can think of no excuse for a speaker being late. All other contingencies should be considered beforehand and be part of the plan.

- **Including too much detail, talking over the heads of the audience**—This is a common mistake of inexperienced speakers, who include facts, details, jargon, survey stats, data, data, and more data, as if this will make the speaker sound smart—usually occurs when the speaker doesn't feel that way.

- **Giving handouts during the presentation**—This common error is done in the belief that by giving the audience something it somehow gives the speaker credibility or legitimacy. It does neither and steals the audience's attention away from the speaker onto the handouts. After giving the audience a handout, good luck getting their attention back!

- **Answering questions during the presentation**—The fact that a question was asked during the presentation indicates a mistake was made by failing to announce beforehand that the audience should hold all questions until the question and answer time.

- **Not maintaining eye contact, turning back to audience to look at audio visual content**—This error is caused by lack of practice time rehearsing with audio visual content.

- **Using inappropriate humor**—There are two problems here. The first is not knowing the audience and the second is the lack of common sense not to use inappropriate humor.

- **Using tired, old clichés**—This is caused by poor, sloppy, inadequate research. It makes the speaker and the subsequent remarks seem irrelevant.

- **Using the quotes, remarks, or comments of others as though they were your own**—Plagiarizing in a speech is just as bad as plagiarizing in writing. This is an error in judgment at best and a shameful lapse in character at worse. In either case, it is an insult to all speakers and all audiences

- **Speaking in a monotone**—This is a bad speaking technique that can be improved with practice and can be avoided with the proper amount of rehearsal time.

- **Failing to give the audience hope or leaving them with what they came to hear**—The audience expects to hear a message that gives them something they can take away—for example, hope, a lesson, an idea, or a memory.

- **Failing to control the question and answer (Q&A) session and letting an audience member dominate it**—This is a result of failing to practice the way to handle the Q&A.

Mistakes of performance are things that don't go right during the execution of a good plan. These are generally mistakes made by inexperienced speakers or things out of the speaker's control. These mistakes are easily corrected, and when they are the speaker's skill and confidence levels both rise. Some mistakes of performance are as follows:

- **Reading too much or depending too heavily on notes and repeatedly getting lost and needing to reestablish eye contact with audience**—This is commonly a result of nervousness and the fear that the speaker will lose her place in the remarks.

- **Mispronouncing a word or two or temporarily stuttering over a word**—This happens all the time to even the most experienced speakers. It is just one of those things the speaker can't dwell on at the time or after.

- **Bringing up a point in the conclusion that was left out of the main body of the remarks**—This usually happens to an inexperienced speaker who wants to make sure he covers that important point he suddenly realizes was left out during the speech. Practice will correct this; don't bring up anything in the conclusion that wasn't previously mentioned.

- **Temporarily losing train of thought**—Just about everyone who speaks has a moment where the mind goes blank. Experienced speakers know it is just a second or two before the thought trail returns. Inexperienced speakers may want to panic—don't. Just take a breath, look for or think about your key safe word, and go from there.

- **Not smiling enough**—This one has to be fixed. Smiling is a critical nonverbal signal that connects the speaker to the audience.

- **Losing control due to circumstances beyond the speaker's control that interrupt the presentation**—This includes power or lighting failure, audience disruption, and audio visual mishap. The only way to learn how to handle these kinds of issues is through experience. In any situation like these remain calm and be a leader.

- **Shifting to negative tone in remarks**—The mistake here is getting caught up in an emotion or feeling and surrendering good sense and control to emotions. When you feel the urge to "join the mob," stop and take a breath and then go back to your prepared remarks.

- **Showing no passion or inspiration**—This is an omission usually caused by fear or anxiety of speaking. It can be overcome by practice.

- **Not using rhetorical techniques**—This is an omission usually caused by fear or anxiety of speaking. It can be overcome by practice.

- **Not connecting with the audience**—This is usually a result of the speaker coming to the podium without smiling and making eye contact.

- **Not allowing voice to fill the audience chamber**—This is usually caused by fear or anxiety of speaking. It can be overcome by practice.

- **Failing to use active but controlled gestures**—This is usually caused by fear or anxiety of speaking. It can be overcome by practice.

- **Not showing leadership during the presentation**—This is most commonly a result of an inexperienced speaker dealing with anxieties about speaking and then being confronted with unexpected circumstances. Natural leadership will arise and manage the situation.

- **Apologizing for mistakes**—Calling attention to your mistakes is unnecessary and a form of self-punishment. The audience does not know you made a mistake. There is no need to make them aware of it and encourage them to lessen their esteem for you.

You Have to Breathe

Many inexperienced speakers make a common mistake: They forget to breathe. In the excitement or anxiety of the moment they launch into their remarks, and in a rush of adrenalin they literally forget to breathe. It sounds odd that you need to be reminded to breathe, but you do. Losing your breath can add anxiety you don't need, and it is easy to overcome by just paying attention to your normal inhalation and exhalation requirements.

Before you are announced and stride to your speaking space, you should take one or two deep breaths, taking air in through your nose and exhaling through the mouth. Focus on the breaths coming from the diaphragm and not the upper chest.

Your remarks are going to run a bit faster than you practiced because your adrenalin is going to be working overtime. So take time to breathe. Try to build in pause moments (you'll have plenty of time).

If you do lose your breath, simply pause (which itself is an effective nonverbal tool), take a breath or two, and then continue. If you want to give emphasis to the pause, bring one open hand to your chest (the take my breath away gesture) and then continue.

Key Takeaways

- If you make a mistake, ignore it. Do not apologize; just keep going with your remarks.

- Some mistakes happen because the speaker didn't plan as carefully as she should have. These mistakes can be corrected by better planning and more practice.

- Mistakes of performance happen during the presentation and are mainly because of inexperience. These mistakes can easily be corrected.

- Speakers must learn to breathe correctly using the diaphragm to ensure they don't hyperventilate or lose their breath during the speech.

8

Step 8: Don't Worry—The Worst You Can Imagine Will Never Happen

In the end, your speech or presentation will turn out okay. You will still do better than 90% of people in similar situations. Remember this: The vast majority of the people in your audience would rather be the person in the coffin than the person giving the eulogy. They can't imagine themselves doing what you are doing. The result of this empathy is they are rooting for you to succeed. You will have a hometown crowd and all the benefits that entails.

Let's examine your worries about what you think could go wrong. Research tells us that the things we worry about almost never occur. About 85% of the things people worry about never occur or, if they do, materialize at about 10% of the level that we thought would occur. In other words, if what we worry about actually does happen, the effects are much less severe than we thought they would be, so we worried too much. Only about 5% of what we worry about ever actually occurs.

When we think about all the horrible things that could possibly happen as a result of our stage fright, we ought to know that realistically these things just are not going to happen.

To help my students and clients visualize this I have them write out their fears. Over the years these fears have included the extremes of dying, passing out, being struck dumb, vomiting, going blind, and going into a coughing fit, as well as the more realistic fears of forgetting the words or losing their place in their notes. (Of course, if you use notes, you will have to break eye contact to refer to those notes. However, if you have practiced your presentation at least six times, you will be able to quickly glance at your notes, find what you need, and regain eye contact with the audience.)

In this exercise I also have my students and clients write down the other extreme—the very best, most wonderful things that could happen. These comments have included standing ovations, wild cheering, unending ovations, and multiple invitations from media outlets to be interviewed. Of course, the point of these exercises is to demonstrate that realistically neither extreme is going to occur, but the most probable situation is something in the middle.

This means the presentation or speech will not be a disaster nor will it likely be completely mistake free—most seldom are. What all speakers need to realize is the audience doesn't know in advance what you are going to say or how you are going to say it. If you make mistakes, only you will know unless you stop to tell them. So don't tell them. If you make a mistake, go right on with your speech, and they will likely never know. If they know or suspect you made a mistake, they still won't be sure, but they will silently respect you more for your grace and pose as a speaker.

Key Takeaways

- The worst thing you can imagine is never going to happen, nor will the best thing you can imagine happen.

- If you prepare as suggested in this book, you will do better than most presenters, and you will be pleased with your performance.

- If you make a mistake, keep going and don't tell the audience. They won't know unless you tell them.

9

Step 9: The Last Thing You Do Is What Most People Will Remember— Do It Well

Every speaker I know is happy when the last words of the speech have been uttered. If you are happy with your effort, you probably want to exit as quickly as possible. However, you might have a question and answer (Q&A) session that follows. In many cases, the audience is also ready for the presentation to be over—not because they were not appreciative of your efforts, but because they are eager to get back to work or head out to lunch and so on. Since you want the audience to remember the last part of your presentation, it is key that the Q&A be a success.

In the vast majority of cases questions will come from people who have genuine, legitimate questions. In some instances a question will be what is referred to as a *softbull* or a question so easy to answer that you can't help but look great answering it. Once in a while there is someone in the audience who thinks he is the smartest person in the room or on the planet and wants everyone to know it. This person will begin a question with some snobbish comment, observation, or quote to establish the fact that he is the genius. This type of person is easy to spot, and his question gives him away just as easily as if he were wearing a flashing neon sign saying "Look, everyone, I'm an arrogant butt-head trying to show off."

These questions frequently begin as a two- or three-part question including some recent source or authority. At this point everyone in the room is annoyed and put off by the person's boorishness. Regardless of which type of person or which type of question you get, you answer them exactly the same way using a three-step model. The three-step approach to handling questions from an audience member is as follows:

1. Acknowledge the questioner by looking at the person who asked the question. It is helpful to take a step or steps toward the person. Listen to the question. Listen for key words or phrases, especially those you are familiar with. Smile all the time.

   If it is a softball question pick out the one or two key words with which you're most familiar and begin to formulate the outline of your answer.

   With long, convoluted, multipart questions, run the key words and phrases through your mind and begin to prepare *your version of the question*.

2. This is very important! Turn away from the questioner and look at another person. Make eye contact, smile, and say, "the question was...," restating the question in a way you prefer to answer. You can shorten it, redefine it, reword it, reposition it, or *recreate an entirely different question*. Remember it's now your question, so you restate it the way you want (see Figure 9.1).

3. Now turn again to a third person, smile, and say, "the answer is...." Then answer the question you created (see Figure 9.2).

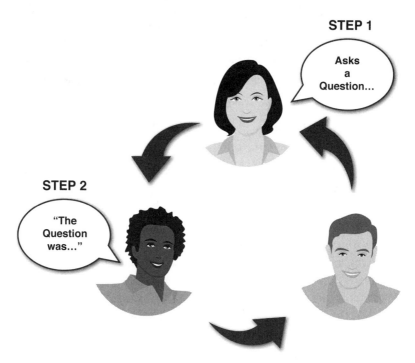

Figure 9.1 How to rephrase the question you want to answer

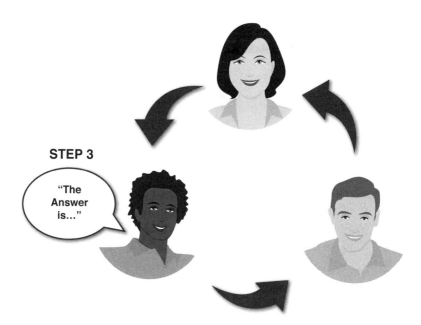

Figure 9.2 How to answer the question you want to answer

Now the important point that keeps the Q & A in your control: *Never, ever* return to the original questioner and ask, "Did I answer your question?" (see Figure 9.3). And never allow that person to get a second question or an additional comment. It is not a dialog between you and another audience member. Too many negative things can occur, including the person saying "no," or "actually, what I really wanted to know was," or "I had a follow-up." Before you know it you are in a two-way competition, and the audience is mad at both of you.

Figure 9.3 That question and that questioner are finished—do not recycle them

Now you can move on the next question, which should be handled in the same manner. At some point you need to look at your watch or feint looking offstage and say "I see we have used up all of our time." Then exit the stage with the same dignity and smile you had as you entered. The last thing the audience sees is what they remember most.

If You Don't Know the Answer to a Question

In spite of the fact that you have done quite a bit of research on your topic, there may be a legitimate question from the audience that you have no clue as to the answer. In this situation, it is perfectly fine to say you don't know the answer, but if it is really important to the person you will try to find the answer and get back to her. Then tell the person to see you afterward to leave her card. Do not ask whether anyone in the audience knows the answer. You still control the speaking space and do not surrender it until you exit.

Your Final Words

Remember, you are still in charge of the platform. You decide when it's time to end. However, if your allotted time is up, it is your responsibility to close down and end the session. Some speakers are all too happy to do this. But some speakers who have just had a successful presentation, where everything went better than they expected and the audience responded exceptionally well, want to bask in the glow of that success. Don't ruin your moment.

Your speech or presentation is probably part of a scheduled event with other speakers, and the schedule must be kept. End on time. Let the audience know that time limitations prevent further questions and comments. If you are available for more discussions, tell them where that would be (that is, outside, online, or via email or text).

To Thank or Not to Thank

Besides whether to use or not to use PowerPoint, the most debated question among speakers and speaking coaches is do you thank the audience or not. The people who support thanking the audience say it's an act of common decency and gratitude that helps build a bond between the speaker and the audience.

The other group says the thank-you makes the speaker look weak. Why thank the audience? The speaker did all the preparation, did all the work, took all the risk, and put forth all the effort. Thanking the audience weakens the speaker's credibility.

I understand both arguments and personally come down more on the "not to thank" side. I prefer to leave my audiences with a strong closing thought that they can ponder long after. A thank-you is so final. It's an end, and I don't want my audiences to feel that way. I want to leave them wanting more.

For relatively inexperienced speakers, you need to do what is comfortable and what seems natural to you. As you gain more experience, you can then decide whether this is an important issue for which you take a position.

Many times following a speech or presentation the host asks the speaker to stay and meet members of the audience. It is important that you accept this invitation for several reasons.

First, you need a decompression, a recognition of completion to give your brain, emotions, nerves, feelings, and unconscious mind the notice that you passed a test—you accomplished something many people never even attempt. This active recognition is more important than you can imagine. People who achieve milestones like this who just put it all away afterward sometimes report days or weeks later temporary sleeping and eating problems and unexplained anxiety. The human body is a complex organism. You can't get it wound up and prepared for something and then afterward just expect everything to be normal immediately. So if there is no official invitation, seek out the event planner or someone else you felt a strong bond with and go have coffee to talk about the topic.

The second reason you should accept the invitation is to say thank you to the person who invited you. It is common courtesy to thank that person. Speakers should get the business card of the person who invited them and anyone else who assisted during the presentation and follow up with a *handwritten* thank-you note.

Third, the invitation to meet the audience is a great opportunity to network with them. Social networking is the most effective technique for building a lifelong collection of people who have a reason to help each other in many ways. Make sure you have a supply of business cards.

In the end, these are all opportunities for you to showcase your skills and leave a lasting impression.

Key Takeaways

- Your question and answer period is likely the last thing your audience will remember about your speech, so it also needs to be strong.

- You have to finish strong and make the Q&A session seem like you choreographed it, which you did or should have.

- Follow the three-step approach in handling questions and your lasting impression will be positive and strong.

- If you don't know the answer to a question, say so and move on.

- Stay in control of your speaking space until you walk away from it.

- You decide whether to thank the audience or not.

- Leave the speaking space with as much grace and poise as when you entered.

10

Step 10: If Any of the First Nine Steps Seem Awkward, You Owe It to Yourself to Ignore Them

Every speaker or presenter is not the same and should not expect to be able to develop and use communication skills in the same way. In other words, use your head and common sense. Not only are no two speakers alike, but not all speaking situations are the same, and not all situations are ideal for some or all of the nine previous steps mentioned in this book. If you practice the steps, become familiar with them, and use them enough so you instinctively know the fundamentals, it is okay to eliminate or modify any of the steps in certain situations. The ability to modify a technique comes from mastering the fundamentals.

What is necessary is you have to try out the suggested ideas and concepts and become proficient in the basics. Relatively inexperienced speakers should not freelance and experiment with things that they have not tried before. I have been doing public speaking for more than 50 years and teaching, mentoring, and coaching communications and public speaking for more than 40 years. I have taken just about every commercial course on the market, read most of the literature, and researched and written extensively on the topic. I have made most of the mistakes a speaker can make, and I am just coming to the point where I feel comfortable with varying some of the traditional approaches.

What is critically important for you now is getting in front of people and practicing speaking on topics you are familiar with and comfortable with. Don't worry about being perfect or what people think of you. If you follow these steps and prepare for your presentation, with a little practice, it becomes easier and easier for you to do successfully.

Index

H

Haiku Deck, 90, 92
half smiling, 53-54
handouts, 86
holding objects during speeches, 116
holding up objects from the podium, 116
home field advantage, combating fear, 45-46
Homo Sapiens, 13-14
humor
    introductions, 73-75
    stage fright, 59

I

"I Have a Dream," 128
importance of public speaking, 1-3
influence, 110
    colors, 92-93
information, organizing, 71-72
information saturation, 71
instincts, amygdala-driven, 6
interactional synchrony, 75
introductions, 72-73, 125
    humor, 73-75
    preparing, 46
isometric exercises, 44

J

jewelry, 12
Johnson, Lyndon B., 21
jokes, stage fright, 59

K

Kazi, Faraaz, 105
Kelly, Kevin, 12
Kennedy, President John F., 70
key points, limiting, 22-23
King Jr., Martin Luther, 81, 128
Kipling, Rudyard, 14, 71
Kirschling, Gregory, 78

L

language
    delivering words in special ways, 20-22
    power of words, 14-20
    technology of language, 12-14
leadership, 110-111
learning to tell stories, 69-70
life experiences, sharing, 83
light from projectors, avoiding standing in, 117
limiting key points, 22-23
Lincoln, Abraham, 21
Luntz, Dr. Frank, 14

M

main body of your speech, 75-76
managing stage fright, 48

McMillan, Don, 89

meeting the audience, 142-143

Mehrabian, Professor Albert, 7

memory aids, 25-26

men, dress, 11

metaphors, 79-80

microphones, 114-115

mind going blank, 49-50

mirror neutrons, 124

mistakes, 127-128

    mistakes of performance, 131-133

    mistakes of planning, 128-130

    during presentations, 43

    worst things you can imagine, 135-136

mistakes of performance, 131-133

mistakes of planning, 128-130

modifying speaking techniques, 145-146

"monkey see monkey do" cells, 124

motor mimicry, 75

N

negativity, avoiding, 117-118

nonverbal communication, 7-8

    body language, 5-6, 99, 119-120

    facial expressions, 6

    first impressions, 8-9

    impact of, 119-120

positive nonverbal signs, 123-124

    toasts, 30-31

not smiling/half smile, 53-54

notes, 85

    examples, 85-86

O

objectives, plans, 10

obstacles to plans, 10

Ockham's Razor, 10

OHP (overhead projectors), 97

organizing your information, 71-72

    conclusions, 83-84

    introductions, 72-73

    humor, 73-75

    main body, 75-76

Orwell, George, 78

    rules of a good communicator, 125-126

overhead projectors (OHP), 97

P

pace of presentations, 116-117

pacing, stage fright, 51-52

panic attacks, 36

pauses, 83

performance, mistakes of performance, 131-133

performance anxiety, 37-38

phrase fillers, 56-57

Pinocchio effect, 121

slides

 creating, 90-92

 tips for using, 95-96

 whiteboards, 96

visual simulation, 18

volume when speaking, 82

 stage fright, 57-58

W-X-Y

walk, 102

walk-through, 102-103

watches, 119

weak legs, stage fright, 58

web content, visual aids, 97

What Technology Wants, 12

when you don't know the answer, to a question, 141

whiteboards, 96

women, dress, 12

word fillers, 56-57

words

 delivering in special ways, 20-22

 power of, 14-20

worry, 40, 135-136

worst things you can imagine, 135-136

wrapping up, Q&A, 141

writing down, plans, 9-10

Z

Zwann, Rolf, 18